The Passions And Pains Behind Her Eyes

By Meka La'Shun

© 2016 by Meka La'Shun. All rights reserved.

Published by Amorous Ink Publishing
Indianapolis, IN 46220

No part of this publication may be reproduced or transmitted in any form or by any means, electronic or mechanical, including photocopy, or any information storage and retrieval system, without permission from the publisher. The only exception is a brief quotation in printed reviews.

Limit of Liability/Disclaimer of Warranty: While the publisher and author have used their best efforts in preparing this book, they make no representations or warranties with respect to the accuracy or completeness of the contents of this book and specifically disclaim any implied warranties of merchant ability or facilities for a particular purpose. No warranty may be created or extended by any persons. The advice or strategies herein may not be suitable for your situation. You should consult with a professional where appropriate. Neither the publisher nor author should be liable for any loss of profit or any other incidental damages, including but not limited to special, consequential, or other damages.

This is a work of fiction. Names, characters, businesses, places, events and incidents are either the products of the author's imagination or used in a fictitious manner. Any resemblance to actual persons, living or dead, or actual events is purely coincidental.

ISBN 978-1-9431590-2-4
Library of Congress Control Number
2016933537

The publisher would appreciate notification where errors occur so that they may be corrected in subsequent printing and/or editions. Please send comments to the publisher by emailing to biz@leftthought.com

Printed in the United States of America

Introduction:
You can find me deep in an imaginative thought. Very much so to say on many daily instances. In intellectual, sometimes exotic poetic images. Not of knowing as to where they come from I simply write from whats deep. The essence of my heart's core down underneath is where you will find me. Lyrics of life, love, and fantasy visions pouring out of me emptying making room for
more and more.
Someone I truly admire whom extremely motivated when inspiring me, kept telling while encouraging me to just allow my mind to be free and let my poetry flow deeply from my heart. So here I am. In this book, I stand with my heart in my hands so to say. In questioning what my heart feels brought about so many eye opening things. Which also challenged me. It intrigued me, influenced, inspired, and motivated me even more so after each and every write I completed solely. There came a point where i knew beyond any doubts that I could have ever gathered, I knew that my desire to write a book this novel of poetry must be born and made a reality. From adversaries, life's challenges and realizing who I was as a person, through my poetry expressions I knew I had to put pen to paper and tell my story. Inspiring other dreamers out there that have somewhat been exactly where I've been or maybe they are still in that place. A place of feeling stuck. In wanting to be heard and understood. Wanting to make a difference.
So in doing that which I set out to in fact do. Through educating myself from the knowing and the wanting of something more. The want for me which had me hungry for it down right starving trying to attain it. Something I felt

which was meant for me it had to be. In searching my thoughts I often wondered when it came about and through really not even knowing it was truly as it was, I just awoke one morning feeling that way. From love and disappointments, reflections and discovery, in locating whom I was and who I am I present to you Meka's Book Of Poetry: The Passion And Pain Behind Her Eyes.

Acknowledgments:
I want to take this opportunity to thank those whom have motivated by inspiring me to go the distance of wherever my heart desired to lead me. To all of you who have supported my hopes, my wishes, everything that I aspired to accomplish in making my dream of being an author a reality. Your continuous follows, admiration's, and analogies I wholeheartedly thank you. I appreciate each and everyone of you for your love and support.
A very special shout out to Jeffery Sanders Sr. for your continued motivating and inspiring ways in challenging when finding me. For seeing something which laid deep. As a result my poetry flows free. Sincerely, and humbly Thank You.

Same Time- Each Time

Lying here I close my eyes. Taking my mental to this distant place. This destination of him and me and how we are, right here in my place of sleep.

Our last encounter I clearly recollect the little ways he simply stirred me. Aroused in our activity, evoking buried hidden emotions.

His gentle arms engrossed around me: my whole physical self, when greeted with the lengthy awaited embrace in such care. The touch of his soft kept hands to my countenance as he tenderly kissed my lips.

Soft spoken intellectual expressions as we communicate in casual conversation. Beautiful ways he examined me as if he was investigating my every line when anticipating I wasn't even inasmuch as.

To sense his masculine scent being just about, I always perceive in wanting that soaked within me, marinating me.

As a perfectionists ensuring I'm nicely evenly seasoned. Baby soft skin from head to "ohh my", very down below. Natural outer layers, down to the very surface. Tantalizing accounts of how our intimately intimate encounters turn me to utter mush.
Pleasant to my touch, pleasingly in agreement with all my erotic senses. The way I turn you on as if activating a switch causing your flow when I'm doing that thing ..oh

yea you do comprehend in having a completely clear idea of "the thing."

Thoughts in depth of how I found "feelings of strong and constant affection" scoping you out as you unclothe. Lying here right here in this sack of ours anticipating, detaining our journey. The expedition in just the travel to simply being laced in our embrace of this firehouse benevolence we make. The glamorous of your skin. No bumps, ridges, or uneven parts as you lay your bare, defenseless, au natural being within me that which belonged to he now belonging to me.

Soft and gentle embraces over every section of my being. Apparently teasing my every desired craving. Tweaking my protuberances with your fleshy muscular taste with a snip pinch from your teeth. Your lips all up my necklace "um yea" I express. For you know all my hot spots and you enjoy hitting them best. Working your way to my lips with sweet in-depth kisses.

Never ever in any hurry you always handle me with care. I'm your fine glass of wine you've partaken like an intoxicating drink. You always take pride when getting your yoni moist and wet. In knowing I will provide you one hell of an amusement ride every single time. Driving my shaft like a test ride is my specialty at best. I do it very well in paying close attention to just the way your hunny pot really makes you feel. Ascending in summation of you for this ultimate ride as I speak to you "umm yeah baby" you know I'm going to take you there.

Taking you inch by inch in and out very slow. Suction up, down and all around. Your gentle hands cuffed in position of your favorite places to be, all over me, my ass, and beyond. Your stroke to the arch of my back as you gently fondle your fingertips up and down right center. You know beyond any doubt that their turns me on. Making my joystick rise in strength growing thick, strong and very long.

Taking of my body in this state of exotic. Such long, hard yet gentle strokes as I'm in this ride of pleasure. Slow then fast, and up then down umm yea baby all around. Insuring you in knowing I'm on this dick for hours. Expressions of Oh yea and I love it just like that. That which turns you on every damn time. Upon completion of my ride you always have this way. A way of not having say a word oh yeah baby I know our way.

All fours ago... My ass high in the air. Awaiting the arrival of my strong, hard, long and oh my very thick standard shaft to change gears into motion. Upon entrance always doing this little squeal making you aware. Oyea your there. There in my secret place of true ecstasy in heaven. In and out the way you do leaves me so breathless. Intoxicating fucked drunk choked. This love drunkenness has me panting. Taking the palms of your hands embracing my back, ass, and shoulders. We both always go for the climax at the very same time. Each and Every time.

Mr Dread Man

There he stood dark, sexy, chocolate ass brother. With dreads to his back all kinky braids and shit. Enchanting brown eyes which speak to her in depth. To express the lyrics his eyes spoke would be those of sweet melodies all their own so to say. The way he spoke with such clarity really knocked her off her feet. With such confidence so sure of himself at introduction. Mesmerized by his smile makes her smile as if she'd just gotten the grandest surprise.

Tall fine ass brother man slender buff build and shit. Broad shoulders made just for embracing perfect in the arms of her. His hands oh my to describe in depth her full examination of dread man's hands left her wanting them inclined in with hers. Just right fingers not to long not to short oh yes just right. His palms would be perfect for the precise cuffing of her round ass she began to think. Lips just juicy finding herself staring as he speaks.

Watching him speak the way his lips move as he pronounces his words and licking those wet juicy things was like a breath of fresh air after waiting to exhale. Bright white smile that match up to those
enchanting brownie sights leaves her speechless. Intoxicating so. At a loss for words she is taken by his presence in his sex appeal standing before her screaming baby come and get me.

Trying to remain focus in listening to him speak her eyes seem to wonder in awe of his nice thick package. As if saying hmm here I am. Finding herself quite pleased at her discovery, she was now biting her lower lip thinking "ooh wee hot diggity damn". Remaining composed in focusing her sight back on to his sight hanging on his every word.

Noticing her examining him head to toe he does this sexy ass chuckle with a grin from cheek to cheek. Licking his cherries he speaks of how he finds her quite reserved and lovely. Batting her lids she smiles with a "well thank you". Nervous as she is she takes her hand to nudge at her earlobe a thing in which she does when one such encounters.

Nervousness and anticipation of merely wanting to just touch him. Noticing he reaches and grabs her hand intertwining, locking his not to short not to long fingers into hers. Perfectly manicured was another turn on she found herself insight of. There's nothing more appealingly sexy than a man that takes good care of his head to toe. Taking her other hand in placement with his other they are now standing hand in hand.

Feeling him slowly pulling her closer she allows herself to let him just to see what those juice's were just all about.

 Cuffing her chin to tilt her head where her lips met up with his seemed magical. Tasting his minty oh so fresh breath was like coming up from holding her breath underneath water. Leaving her breathless. The way he kissed with so much passion running his fingers those fingers to her cheeks as he pulled her in for more of the kiss. She hadn't been kissed like that in a very long time.

The passion, heat and desire from want all laid behind that one in depth kiss. Deciding in that being enough for this encounter she nicely shy's herself away looking at him ravishingly. Showing those whites and licking those cherries he politely asks so when can I see you again. She coy like replies oh let's see. He then in that moment grabs her in such an embrace kissing her deeply full blown. She's kissing this man as if feasting at the dinner table on a Sunday afternoon.

Sunrise

Embarking on a brand new day the sun makes it's way out of hiding.

Sparkling such rays of bright light in depth of being simply beautiful.

Full of wonderful aesthetic colors lighting up our horizon in full.

A aurora in the break of day when noticed is nothing more than gorgeous.

Poetry To Each Soul

He hits her core with such depth. Awakening desires that have long awaited. Touching her soul with his fingertips leaves her breathless. Beneath him and wants of more and much more. Loving her threw his erotic ways has her drifting to far away places of forever never land.

Feelings of passion and lust consumes her as if seeing an aurora. A very natural electrical phenomenal feeling. He has her raptured and captured in her feelings of what feels oh so good. Feelings which he indeed also feels. An awareness of her body by the way he makes her feel. A emotional state of reactions of a basic physical sense in which her sensations are consciously responsive. Very aware. Any wonder, worry, or suppose with him no longer exist in the way he touches her core is in fact the proof.

Built walls are broken and images unleashed for in him she's a lengthy open book. A book that was once closed for a very long time. Pages withstanding all tests in times time. Opening of said book he reads what lies deep, what's in between each and every line. Upon his readings he learns such knowledge in knowing is the essential component in catching her heart. Learns of every pain from heartfelt hurts. Letdowns and disappointments therefore vanished. Closed mindedness now open to all which surrounds.

A mirroring image of himself is what he finds in her. Alike him in many ways has him in fact captured within her. She takes him to another dimension. One of 3D. His heart, soul, and desires opened in every since. He as she are in fact open novels of sweet poetry to each souls.

A Very Blessed Woman

Waking up to the morning light. I wake from a deep sleep a little confused. Rolling over on my pillow I see the orange like brightness from the sun making its way out of hiding through my window in my place of sleep .

In realization that it was a brand new day I became immediately thankful for my gift in being able to have and share another beautiful unpromised day with those I hold dear and close within my life. I'm thankful for those that entered and exited my life as well. I'm truly very thankful for the beautiful people I have in my life that makes my life worth living. Those special ones that see what lies beneath.

See my dream was somewhat deep. I seldom have these deep in depth mini series of visions and feelings, created by my imaginative thoughts, however when I do I notice all my surroundings in a very detailed way. More detailed than usual. So with determination, motivation, and inspiration I am driven to making this day. Very thankful to my lord for all the ways he blesses me each and every day.
A very blessed woman

What She Missed in Intimacy

The smell of his skin like fresh laced musk sprayed for the sample on trying out in a very exquisite boutique. A scent of sophistication . His soft embracing touch as if she's the only inamorata in his cleverness when you're much dear. Regarded in deep affection, cherished very near. His stride and speech has this way, very long and decisive as carefully laid in detail. One can tell education is of level. Sophisticated, Educated brother unbiased is duly noted.

Words spoken truly in out pour; as flowing rapidly in a steady stream with such depth and compassion. In fact much such knowledge in every way no doubt. Those chestnut brown scoping which are very hypnotizing leaving her in a state of hypnosis. A trance that mesmerizes leaving her dazed for what feels like daily encounters. Monday, Tuesday, Wednesday, Thursday, those no lie are the days in which she would day dream of simply being near just to share the air he breathes.
Friday, Saturday and in count of Sunday those days she's in deeper depth of fantasy. Imaginations away from her running profoundly threw her cerebrum. The brightness of his person and seriousness in his tone when he's in full blown expression really turns her on. His strong mental encounter in which he's very experienced, takes her to a destination of much higher learning.

Strong intellectual in-depth conversations, informal talks with much discussion. Waiting for responses from ultimate passions through declarations. Not beneath however with him, in every way intertwined and there by locked. Valuing her inserts on serious importance exhibits the utmost in regard of strong admiration. Self-esteem not like any other, a confidence in pride and in dignity. Chocolate city fine ass brother. Similar to she as can be.

Thoughts of him come to heart running through her oh so free. When alone heavy inside her whole grain of thought. No visibility from said outsiders she sees from that a far. Beautifully treasured moments of intimacy she really miss the most.

A Cherished Friend

Back in a time when things were simple. When worries were what now seem petty. Fusses over what to wear and of how you were to make it to the very near Friday social. Saturday nights were special too because those were the nights she got to see you.

More aged than she, she saw him as cute and so divine. See her infatuation was kept quite secret. Every time in imagining him it was evidently clear she had her scopes on wanting him. In the know that he was her fondest passion, he was always so very ardent. Youthful love letters she wrote him many, being very persistent he received them each. Full of admiration which were deep-seated felt, he always excepted each and every one. Although in the blistering posterior of her memory scan, she often marveled if in fact they got trashed.

Years went by three to four exact. Their lives they each had indeed subsist. She a Jr., and he having had graduated three years in past. One tolerably cool day after session, while trolling home she sees him, her crush from past.

Caught up in in-depth converse residing of the ages past, in how he had been wishing if she'd only been wiser. Wiser being of the legal age. Four years difference she then sixteen, as he was the full age of in fact twenty. Sightings of her letters verbatim had her two shades darker of the color red. Pondering oh my she was such a silly in youth girl.

Life yet again seem to forcefully intervene, living life's journeys as did he. Seventeen ages later at family gatherings, their paths seem to cross each yet again. In one innocent enticing phone call two lives were forever altered. Intellectual dialogues very in- depth they found themselves having both now in which very mature. "Adult"

Mutual respect for each others livelihood formed an ever lasting bond in them. A bond of love, respect and deep-seated friendship filled with kindness and much goodwill.

Thoughts of how if things were different only made their relationship prosper. Several years now best buds they've been. Fore he has become one of her dearest friends. A friend in him she cherishes still.

The Climax

He says it's a process baby. Break the rules do whatever. You seem to be past due for some sexual healing and I except in being thee that takes u their. Hunger in her eyes she knows she wants this man and every damn thing he is offering. She wants him to take her in his wings and break her walls down. Break her with benevolence. He's already doing this number on her mental and her body oh my the thought of what he will and can really do to her body leaves her breathless. It's consuming her thoughts.

Finding herself caught up in the heat she embarks within. Umm it's hot. So moist and wet from the want and anticipation of thoughts how she wants to have this man from sun up to sun down. The exhilarating emotional state in thinking about him merely touching her makes her kitty umm ten times more hot she feels. The heat to her honey pot like flames over the palms of her hands. Here lying dazed excitingly amazed at this pleasure bestowed upon self from play. Toying with her softness slowly then fast back and slow going mad like a lioness caged for a decade wanting out! She for she oh she wants out. Her mind is far away at this point oh how she's all in her feelings emotional like of how she didn't sign up for this kind of loneliness. She's suddenly blindsided with this deep unconnected feeling an emotion of loneliness which makes her even more moist.

Panting and moaning breathing harder at this point. Taking her joints like sockets moving them up and down and all around visioning this man putting in time taking her deeply. In her thoughts he's grabbing that apple pulling it up as he enters her stronger and farther she squeals "oh my" as she foresees she's about to burst off like a volcano erupting lots and lots of rich thick lava.

Motionless still twirling the pearl bursting before herself she gives into the feelings of enjoyment going in for an even more primal Intense climax that which she's shooting for. She wants that sentiment of erupting till she has no more lava to push out of her motionless, parched, starving very hungry whole physical self.

Animal instincts kicked in and has taken rule. She's panting and moaning near convulsions in explosions just completely taken by this orgasmic ride of pleasures in an outbreak of uncontrollable breaks. She squeezes her hips and grasp her thighs as she's into this volcano for a blow of a lifetime. She's about to pour. Broken. Her walls are at that instant beneath. Gone. Doing so she blurts out oohs and ahhs .. Yesssss that's it right there! Ummm yeah baby that's it right there as she experiences her earth shattering CLIMAX

Intimacy

Yummy baby if I told you that I wanted to sex you in a variety of delicious flavors. With rainbows being my favorite would you allow me the taste of you.

Would you allow me to do so with strong fun benevolence so gentle, and sweet as our souls meet.

See I'm a woman who wants and oh baby umm many yearning needs.

I so need an awakening of your masterpiece inside mine intertwined all so fine.

We would be so in lock down in need of a key. The magic the fire we shall make. Completion, devotion, the intimacy as one.

I'm Awakened

I hereby am awaken to another beautiful not promised day. A new day in beauty of it's everything. The way the light from the sun beaming through as it continues its rise.

The beauty in the trees in their stillness. To the beauty of nature period.

Actually taking the time in noticing and hearing the birds chirp as I begin my journey of living another blessed day.

Noticing all the cars as they drive by with people on the go of a set plan in making this day.

Yes thank you thank you for another day.
Motivation,Determination,& Purpose. A day of purpose!

Love y'all
 Be blessed
Meka

A Fantasy (Vision)

Have you ever had an out of body experience. In which upon you awakening you had a gathering, somehow you been here before. A series of thoughts, feelings and visions. Normally occurring in dark fall. However not questionable in daybreak.

Refreshed by dawn in purpose. Determined in just doing. Simply being. Thereby attained and awoken with such ambitions, aspirations and ideas. Designs of embarking to widely extent, long-lived atmospheres. A Specific Blueprint of one being. You. And yours!

Venue's of desire to acquire instruction in your environment. Your area of land which is controlled by our groups who make decisions for our way of living our private capitalism. To in fact wake knowing your part in the journey is to be a part in something for the greater good.

Embodying intellectual conversations in which acquire you to think logically. In which taking involvement in serious studies and energy gathering, earnest thoughts. Thoughts which embark you to destinations in a later time in of beyond. Beyond where your thoughts have ever gathered.

Sheer educational feasting of the brain. There's power in knowledge. Found knowledge brought about through enlightenment. Enlightenment welcomed and taken to hand by a fantasy (vision).

A Moment In Time

He calls me with sweet talks of intimacy. Oh how he wants the depth of me. He speaks sweet lines of poetry to my soul. He wants to be the ink in my pen and the paper that I write my flows of poetry on to so he says.

Suppression is done to prevent the development, action or expression of something. Lock it away and as with him that's what was done. This man in one intimate phone call has made me feel vibrations and waves like an overflowing ocean ready to come in from a big tide...a regular movement both at an upward and downward level caused by the pull of his sun and my moon on our earth..the flow of my ocean as the tide rises and falls is the height he has me on.

It's always been him he says metaphorically meaning it's always been me. Rehashing sweet young adolescent memories I'm taken. Taken back to the moment in time on the stairway of an auditorium when and where it was just him and I.

 He wants to take me there it's very evident and is doing an excellent, very successful job in executing.
 All I want is that shot with you he says, you know that shot before you ran oh way back when. Taking me back to the stairway yet again. I know you remember that kiss we shared. It was as if my world stood still. Again I just want my chance to share your space, the air you breath let me be your air baby.

Listening to him speak with so much passion and declaration has me twisted and turned in so many directions therefore altering me clearly thinking. Who was he to come at me this way rehashing a long ago moment in time. I was torn between things I remembered from the stairway and things I suppressed. There I was again stuck on the intimate kiss. Thoughts of thee which made the tuck away memories slowly come to head. The way he touched me kissing my neck to my lobes and down to my breast. Dazed and babbling oh why did I tuck this away why on earth would I?

He says boo I want to be your end of the day. Your end of the week for that matter too. I've been on the sideline of this game with you far too long I want my chance in. Won't you let me into your lane I promise I will not sway into another. It's always been you since that kiss in the stairway of the auditorium oh so long ago. Allow me to be your motivation and inspiration in this novel of write you've expressed in depth. Baby just let me be. Let me be the water you drink that quenches your thirst at the end of a very intense work out we share.

In ties and knots my insides began to churn. Shit! I am thirsty lioness on a hot summer's day at this point. Here he was reciting not only my love for poetry when I realize his love for poetry to the very core. Stirred and shaken I am speechless. Still on the doubt and uncertainty in knowing why in the fuck did I not allow myself to feel, show or be affected by you.

In that thought he expresses brown eyes you suppressed it out of fear. I was older when I told you I loved you and you weren't ready. You asked me if I was upset because you didn't feel the depth of my passion that resided in my heart for you in yours. Baby that sweet tender moment all those years ago you were and should have been mine. Respecting your wishes I let u run. Love can't you see. That was our moment in time.

Departure

What was this emptiness she felt inside. Was it him or was it she. How was it they couldn't seem to get it right. Not wanting to lose a friend coming to the conclusion that she would be better off as would he. Going from never wanting to see it end to here let me help you pack your shit! From I love you baby to ooh wee I can't tolerate your ass!

A love that once was so damn real, suddenly before your eyes is not the deal. At one moment in time the best of friends. Now complete strangers basically roommates. Their was a time she would tell him everything and anything. Now keeping secrets about the stupidest of things. How could the very oath they stood to take became the vows they each would break. It's been said sometimes people grow apart, and as with them this was the case.

To love, honor, cherish is what they said. For better, worse, in sickness or health till death did them part is what the preacher man read. It's what they said. Here it was the break and all they could muster was hate, dishonor, and pity. We are living a lie she expressed to him as tears formed and stream down her cheeks. As he was in denial in the saddest of ways. He loved her however had no love for self. And here she was had been loving him and had lost her love and respect for self. Why did our love have to change was constant in her brain. What happened to their magic made.

The best relationships to the naked eye aren't as perfect

behind closed doors. There are hurts, disappointments, secrets deep dark secrets and dishonesty too. Here were two people which seemed to be as perfect to all their friends. When In all actuality were not so perfect. Each had been hanging by a dangling string. Walking on crated egg shells. Acting their love out. Playing pretend. Trying to hang on to what was gone. Doing the best they could she for him and he for she.

Late nights all alone missing what they had. Remembering when she could just lie her head hearing his heartbeat. Remembering when their heartbeats were in sync. Remembering the last words he said. You hate me and I hate myself for not being your man. I messed up baby my heart beats for your love and I don't know how to give it. So many tired cries left unheard and deeply shed. Insecurities got the best of them and now there they were just through.

Lying in her bed she seldom thought how everything she use to vision and everything she use to be only reminded her of things they went through. Memories of how their love would've conquered all if time would somehow had frozen still. Time stands quiet for no one realizing now she must have been brain frozen crazy as hell. Knowing now he couldn't love her right as she couldn't return the benevolence in full depth. For she desired a different love. A benevolence in oneness and fun affection for self. Some reevaluating had to be done.

Oneness..one must love self before another. In doing so

locating and embracing a new profound in depth love within. Full of challenges of self which drove her into better. Feeling better than she's ever felt. All from the scars and hurts left behind. All from the wounds that bout drove her mad insane. Prevailing her love for self all which stemmed from the heartaches in departure.

Before You I Stand

Before you I stand dark skinned one would call chocolate brown sugar whose meek, delicate and very sweet to meet. Words I speak run out of me like water as my soul has learned to speak. Telling stories of self life and learned lessons threw my scan of memory. With purpose and drive, motivation and determination I strive to rise. Rising above any level I have lived past hurts and pains on my journey of being better.

Driven by struggle with the mentality that my life is my life and what I make of it ultimately defines me and my determination being constant. Quitting is not in my game plan as I have this reoccurring dream of going the distance as my mental and physical mind takes me.

I stand here in existence having gave life to five to be exact. My hearts and souls that I drive with influence to be all they want to be in this one life I blatantly express that they have. There are no shortcuts, no hidden corners to coward behind as these are your lives I can reflect back on always preaching.

Determined to teach that quitters never prosper in winning in this game of being. Driven by a goal set to raise my boys to be successful black men that take care of what's theirs letting nothing or no one ever stand in between. Raising my girl to excellence of a fruitful life which with goals and aspirations of being just whatever it is that she decides to be. As I am and will take no excuses as to why the best can't be given. Depend on no one but self as independence has no shame.

 The road has been bumpy but still rise each awakening day with a new strive in motivation to get them there. In this which before you I stand.

A Place From Prayer

In Moments where I wanna break by just separating myself into a thousand parts and pieces from the set backs and behaviors, the adaptations of life. The attitudes and respect lack of or of just plain in cognizance; I travel to a place of quietness, somewhat of a deaden. I know it's a incredulity an area of darkness brought on from a position of pain. When I'm at this place of dismal; one will acquire distance and an irritable quietness, as which I will and do become discomposed.

I engage myself in prayer and as a result I am therefore in a state of tranquil: quiet but peaceful. Because to engage in negativity is toxic: causing poisonous substances. Fore defeat is in my mind, and Resilience is in my soul. Starting where I stand; In courage I find a wisdom that life is funny with its curves and corners, as thru time I have really learned sometimes in some occasions a hurt turns about when at a chance of winning had I stuck it out.

When low times call tempting me to answer; offering me free housing I have a choice to make. To go upward securely, joyfully, and swiftly on my path of prudent happiness or take the hill downward with all its stresses and pains. I choose the ways of upward embracing A Place From Prayer.

A Reflective Thought

What do we gather from each day we partake. Is it love for others as well as self. Maybe its compassion and empathy in others experiences on another level higher than our own. Can we imagine the projections of others in a mental state. A state of which we are infused with them. Infused meaning:
To introduce one into another. So as to affect it through out.

In all representation can we bring to them a deeper signification of the topics at hand. Motif being "UNSPOKEN WORDS & TRUTHS UNTOLD". Who or what will we or they become from the lessons at hand. We are all trapped in a maze "our generation" with no way out. We are locked in a room "our minds" with no light. Experienced enough to know the degree by which things differ and still we choose to not do what's right.

 Why are we at battle "fighting" among each other for the exact "demand" in rights that we all deserve. When will we realize that we all bleed Red, What lies beneath is truly what's deep. Really our fate is what we make.

When did I love you's go from meaning I love you into what can I get from you. Committed relationships go from being based on Trust, Honor, and Respect, as well as love; to One Night stands, Friends with Benefits, Side piece nigga's and bitches too. Really what kind of honor lies in being a friend with benefits. So how do you knowingly call yourself this. Where's the respect for self in doing such disaster. Where is the love, passion and commitment gone to in this day.

When did we stop believing that together we stand, divided we fall. When did we become a people of so much hate for ourselves as well as others.

We need to be loving one another as well as ourselves on a deeper respect level. A level of knowing who we are, what we are, what we want from this life we are living. We need to cease the moments and we need more Go Getters. Go get what you want out of life because no one is giving you anything in this life. Life is what we make of it.

This is merely my intellectual concept on things that plague my mind. Things that I think hard about and feel with passion on. I come from a place of peace with this write. I can be doing other things and something hits me to speak on. Sometimes I can make sense of it and put it all to write, and other times I can't even find the words to express in depth the just of what I'm thinking. I hope this touches someone in a way of enlightenment as I ending it completely enlightened.

Integrity vs Character

A way of being where you do what
you express you are going to
when you were in the mood you were
in when stated.
Not just to hear yourself speak or
to say you even spoke it.
Not possessing those said ways in your
lies and being proud like when boastfully
expressing as though bragging it makes you unaccountable.
Unreliable. Not trusting with a pure.
Which in itself is what purity looks for
in accepting by gathering them as friends
or whatever the relationship is.

To stand back. Listening, watching,
 taking full page notes of things that
define whom you are. This verse
 you strongly hold onto, as you with
charm, in between the lines tear down
 those you see below you, calling them
your equals.
You see an intellectual and very mindful in mind setting
ways
Quietly observes.
In notice
Of all those ways.
That defines you.
As if looking in a dictionary to
search the meaning of you.

One of intelligence takes notice
well.
Listening by watching carefully at the things
one does. Little sly ass sneaky ways
the way one will tend to change things to
suit their own needs before those of others.
Ones will lie and defy. Devoted to admitting their
Christianity.
Really!
Actions don't meet up with that
analogy.

Being as it is and that as it may.
Those ways which will come to head
some day.
The Integrity of your being will
carry you long ways,

When examining your character
it plays right along with integrity.
Your character is in all ways the definition of you. What
makes you who you are.
Your set of qualities that make you different from any other
being .Your character is defined
In the ways you treat others to the many ways you in fact
interact with others.
Have you ever knew another which babbles
on and
on and
on some more. Until you are
almost blue in the face.

To wonder, do they really have
 a clue.
In your discovery, realizing no
as a matter-of-fact they do not.
Due to something expressed in the elaborate drawn out
babble that defined who they were to their core.
These are the analogies from a mindful mind. Set in
observing the many ways. In which
 Integrity vs Character.

So Gone

Come baby stimulate my mind and my body into great possibilities of love making just u and me alone. Um you smell quite nice . The smell of a man's cologne is intoxicating. Touching me he pulls me closer leaving me mesmerized as I am taken into this abyss of his love completely lost in this heat of fire he makes.

Taking me kiss by kiss. Gentle stroke by gentle stroke I'm losing it, I've completely lost it. My mind is like mush fore I can't think speak or better yet baby I can't move. So lost in this passion session you have taken me to a new height of ecstasy . My entire world is spinning as if on a merry go round. With every turn around I and my body's taken to this new level of fire and desire. Deep steady penetration strokes like a piano being played key by key gentle strokes as my piano is quiet virgin .

My world is engulfed like a big wave coming to shore ready to run over drowning me into complete ONENESS. Loins aching, biting, pinching, scratching, clawing calling moaning in heat in complete hunger mode ready to feast on every inch of this rock hard steady drive. Embracing my heat piece by piece taking me to a level of eroticism never experienced on the universe of my livelihood. Erotic ways of ummms and ahhhs and umm yea baby's. It's thanksgiving fore I'm so about to feast on my meat til the very last drop completely leaving my plate empty no scraps.

A yummy delicacy the body of my stud is as I partake the sweetness of his Popsicle pool stick gently so in a personal manner. Fore its mine belonging to me to do with play with as I please. Taking its swollen love Stroke by yummy stroke slow steady fast breaking threw my core my memories so far gone. Drifted to this place of beyond this fellow makes me find such I've never fathomed locating.

Going downtown of my nature feasting my peach to flowing dripping juices from his now all so wet lips. Nurturing me Near sprinkle its pre making sure I'm pleasured in 101 different delicious flavors our fire is like whoa as I am Dazed and amazed into them hazel eyes I am therefore gone.

The Lover in She

Allow me to illustrate the passions which lie beneath. To enlighten oh and clarify the benevolence in affection, personal, and related ties. Let's just take it "Downtown" a notch of what makes she simply she.

Her whole new world grounded from love of self, prayer, and laughter as you will find the lover in she. A little was all needed far partaking of this lifestyle she has mentally embraced completely. Although she has patiently awaited to be set free to release her sweet poetry. To go the distance of that what captures; having have waited due to life's unbalance, That which captures the Heart in she. She has been lost and she's endured the lonely she has been saving the lover in she.

Moving mountains among the stars awaiting one to take in time to deeply care. All the madness hushed by existent duties, challenges and such. Affections more so than she can bare, she trusts what she feels when knowing what's right, very understanding rare and tender. A hell of a Lioness hear her roar. She thrives on her faith in hopes she leads a path to follow. She wants her place in the sun.

A river of love is in her hands her light shines bright for she is free. Having learned from past mistakes she accepts where she's at in making the best of each promising rising day. What ever will be with she will just simply be. As if walking anew not allowing life's weights to measure a place on she. Her life gets heavy then there comes that river in love, and hope and yes faith. She sometimes wonders if this beating organ which resides within her chest knows what's best having constantly dealt with the immature drive by's of lurking eyes.

Value she brings having being kept and hidden in a safe haven deep within. A buried treasure surfaced from the bottom of what feels good. She stands tall fore she does not accept defeat from the raging war within, which she is prepared to beat. She desires another to take on the cause not suspecting a loss at all. To see the pains within beneath to stand between it and she. In finding the answers in her ways of love; the hurts past her giving it half a chance; in so doing you will find that the she is me and that I am the lover in she.......

Family

We converse and chill while relaxed. In doing so we are therefore chillaxed. Talks of life and living , with memories of past endeavors from way back when. Intellectual conversations about the world around us. Laughs, Cries, Enjoyments in the presence of one another. We each have one another like no other for we are in fact common kinfolk. A house, line, stock, and tribe comprising our families as one that we are. A tie that's bounded throughout times time.

 Any and everything yes we do discuss from sun up to sun down on occasions when bombardments of life don't. Intervene. Not allowing life's impediments to come between. Whatever goes on in each life we always make time to come as one. Never tired or bored in each others company we each come from a very long line of very positive and loving influences. A generation in young versions of our mothers, mothers, mother. And our Fathers, fathers, father.

Our bodies of living beings constituting single steps in the line of descent from our ancestors. A class of development from an earlier time.
Persons in earlier moments we were descended "originated" from. A long ancestral line of strength, encouragement, aspirations, motivators and strong benevolence from past times and dimensions. Each beautiful in our own unique way we are family in every way…

Dedicated to my Family❤

Promises Of Tomorrow

Can we wander and just converse embracing past what we can devoid in this love that we each do partake. Just what this passion we've partaken within each really does mean in what we are through devotion. How mad that we've ran from this that's rare but pure and honest. U lovingly cover me yielding me from pains pain. We have both waited patiently on this desire neither of us have ever came to be fully complete. How have we managed to stop the fight to find this benevolence of all time.

We love surprisingly unselfishly is it we are meant to be. It's a new meaning when set so free. I'll care for you completely all the way for you bring into me a quiet nocturnal peace that's resided so deep. From me you will find that I do see what your heart's been asking through perseverance. As in you I do indeed find that you are what I have been yearning.

Your declaration in depth to me clearly sets my soul so free. Unleashed you've captured me. To go all the way with you is my oath of attachment with every fragment of my character. You promising a commitment till the end of times time. Your promises to keep me within I lovingly except with such forbearance as I have never been of such.

 To have and hold you are my gifts to this honor fore I see what your heart has been asking. My benevolence is such a good thing the sweetest thing you've ever had you express in me. As you will nurture me for all seasons as you have been hankering your love specifically for me. I really can't call it although I can declare from a place within that each and every day I will love you still.

Deeply I thank you for loving me. You've hereby saved me. I was so lost and lonely and their you came offering me your light and pathway to follow. You light up my life in this now new beautiful world within you. You are the lyrics of my heart and the last breath of my soul. I have been saving my whole being just for you.

Since time was young and earth was new your pledging yourself anew. Wanting to love me all the days of my life if I can withstand. You say to me long before waterfalls from rain and before winters turned into springs you were nearby declaring your soft side in this passionate benevolence meant for me. Fore time stands steal in this creation we share.

You creep past my hurts in wanting me to just allow you to take care of me. All it will take is some participation and elevation in letting it flourish and fruitfully blossom. You want to be here beside me all the days of my existence and all you ask is for me to simply be. You make what's fake seem so real. The perfect start to a dark day. Like I'm moving only I'm standing still. It's all about me and you and our promises from yesterday stumbling through today leading us into tomorrow.

Black Is Simply Beautiful

Beautiful brown mocha toned goddess, flawless in the way she glows. Skin soft like cotton to the gentle touch like somewhat of a feather. To look into her shine is magnificent. Each line finely designed to each crescent curve. Radiance which beams like the horizon on a beautiful crisp bright morning. The lining of her light from the source of the sun shining so bright. Her curves the way they felicitously are in agreement with the lining in the formal that she exhibits.

Her pose like that of no other, with such confidence being intoxicating breathtaking. The swerve of her hips as she takes her position is divinely one of exquisite taste. Extremely divine and typically delicate, lovely and elegant in every way. Such flawless posture which unequivocally suggest a mature contended, very satisfied perfectionists.

Merely having all God given qualities in which she proudly possess. She's simply immaculate, picture-book perfect, impeccable in all said characteristics. Her special trait which makes her distinct from any other in existence. Reality is she's coincidental in each of her precise ways. Nothing added, nothing extra, she is in fact an actual in the duration of this time.

Graceful she is delightful, she's a primal example that which proves beyond any shadow of doubt that Black is Simply beautiful.

Open Mind/Open Heart

What do you gather from an amid awakening. An awakening from a mere enlightening experience. An experience in which unbelievably you feel you see things so much clearer. Always one of believing in those visions chosen ones only see. All your years idly on standby in notice of all those called way before you.

Seeing the light as old wise tales would speak. Stone crazy and done lost one's mind the young would've told. Simple mindedness blind ones can't hear the spirit speak. When saw, your mental is of awoken, to everything around you. Breathing it, living it in everyday endeavors. As if awakening anew. New being, new life, and experiences, and adventures too. Seeing the good in all, taking life's hurdles as they come, existing in the knowing that one day their time will come. Entering into the now and leaving the then behind.

Brand new days to get it right. In thankfulness of each rising day, taking each as they come. Taking each sun risen horizon, as seconds to minutes and minutes to hours, counting them singly each per each. It's not a holy ghost way or type of such. What it is in fact is knowing. It's simply in the knowing.

Take yourself out on a limb and open oneself up all the way, to all which surrounds you, in your everyday living in existent. So many good God fearing people I have so encountered, that has entered my life or exited leaving fingerprints on my being. God fearing ones, you know them in their everyday ways of life. In the things they do and say, hell the way they simply be. You have the fellow that's a family man, it absorbs him like water to sand, when watching him with his most prized possessions, his kids the precious ones. Sit back and really see the respect he has for his mom. In that alone shows you he's in fact an enlightened one. The love that lies behind his eyes when looking into those of his wife. Respect so much it out pours from his every being. It's in his every way of walk, talk, and gesture. Indeed a pure at heart. Focus in on the one that you're always seeing doing of good deeds those by choice of their own are indeed the ones chosen. Always trying to help out another in way of job opportunity, lending of ends, borrowing of such, any and everything is just in fact their way. Not doing in way of notice... ie... to be seen or say "yea I helped him out". Those in fact are the chosen, the one's that touches my very existence.

On the flip side you have the ones that just can't get it right even when they try. You know the one's that lie looking at you. Everything and every way of being is all deceitful. Their dark so it oozes all over everything they possess. Their presence is toxic. To be around them is a noticeable consumption that it takes something away from you. You know the lurking eyes which will steal you blind of all your goods and joy. The guilt stricken so to speak that think their shit don't stink. Those are the one's we must show, that's just not the course to lead. By living the paths we live.

In our everyday life's lessons we partake a divine path to leadership, encouragement, and ownership. In doing so we are the living proof that with an open mind we each do have very open hearts.

Ideological Soul Mates

What if he and she really were meant to be.
What if when man made he, the he made
was in fact made for she. When making he
all of his physical traits being; brown eyes,
dark hair, baby soft skin, gleaming white smile,
what if all those traits were outlined just for she
and vise versa.

Let's put that into deeper thought.
What if she was designed just for he. Her eyes,
smile, nose, mouth and all the essential elements
that made her outer, was aligned just for the meeting
of he. Let's say their hearts were so in tune that they
both beat to the same rhythm. Their souls were so
in sync that she held the lock and he dangled the key.
What if they two were perfectly suited for the other in
perfect temperament. Moods, attitudes even behaviors.
What if they were simply temperamental.

All their lives each has wondered, practically
marveled at the notion that out there's that
one other being designed especially for each.
Its pretty deep in fact to envision. Astrologically
people are linked up all the time by their signs.
Astrology is in fact the study of how the positions
of the stars and movement of the planets have a
supposed influence on the lives and behavior of people.

Duly noted that zodiac sun signs are grouped

into four essential ingredients that when combined,
create the world and allow life to flourish.
Said each of those twelve astrology signs fall under
a specific component and the four factors help in
understanding everybody's place in the world.
That being said it's possible for he to be designed
especially for she.

That from the horizon in the sun and the placement
of the moon that it's unequivocally possible for
two individuals to be truly in depth meant to be
in coexistence. Existing together in actuality at the
same time. But if we are coexisting definitely
out lined in complete alignment with one such state,
Isn't that in fact called fate.

Fate now to examine fate. The power that is believed
to control what happens in the future. The will in fact,
principal, or determining cause by which two people
in general are believed to come to be as they are or
events to happen as they do.
It's Inevitable, Kismet, and Predetermined.
Thereby making it possible for he and she
to be Predestined Ideological Soul mates.

Inspirational Inspired

Driven by a passion to have more in this life I am living, I have encountered a strong sense of knowing that my life is indeed no doubt just that which I have declared. Seized by an obsession, I made a conscious decision from within, to step from behind the walls I myself built, to fully flourish out from hiding showing all my Godly given capabilities in being the very best I can be. Delighted at my very creation in the knowing that I was and am here with purpose. Determined from that reason to simply locate, educate, therefore fuel by feeding my intellectual ideas. Enthralled with expression I openly communicate my fondest tho deepest examined evaluations when declaring my out pours in my artistic writes. Entranced by vision in seeing and believing that I too can in fact be exactly what I aspire to be. A self-proclaimed
writer.

Diverted by daydreams which keeps me in focus of my goals that will come to birth allowing me to embrace all that I am with full potential of simply being. To be among the very few who dare to follow their dreams from within the lover in me.

Filled with emotions that consume by motivating me in my everyday ways of living. Never giving in to doubt when Life's challenges arise. As they do tend to subsist. Fueled by compulsion, a very strong nocturnal desire to do what was in fact truly destined just for me.

Consumed with beauty way past I can see, all which stemmed from my aggressive mentality for wanting to know and simply be more. My want to merely see in completely educating me. In me I am truly unequivocally driven within my determination in being inspirational which is something within that makes me want. Giving me these ideas, leaving me influenced and deeply inspired.

Complete

It had been one of them damn days. All she could think of was getting to her domicile and call it a day. To lavish in the night's darkness sounded seemly in-fact. With thoughts to intake a nice ice cold glass of the finest wine after which. A before thought reasoning oh how it would be so nice to be laced up in embraces with Mr. If only!

Images of all the many enjoyments that would be in occurrence from dusk to dawn. Oh my. If only. The stalwart desire yes a great physical power, to be exclusively, nothing more than, taken. Carried, Moved, or Lead, to what seemed like a far away place. The emplacement of said he and she. Her strong mental simply takes rule two glasses after intake, and she takes on her pen for a sultry, very elegant juicy write.

The closure of her eyes brings about the image she needs of having him right there. Pretty brown scopes, dark brown hair, masculine build. Broad ass shoulders biceps of such that really turns her on. Sweet tasting lips, she licks her lips in thought of. Enchanting smile which lights up her life. Before him biting her lower lip as he indeed would know exactly just what she was thinking. Awoke she is very, daydreaming only its night, of all in which she could be doing with her Mr. If only he were there.

To in-fact have him, simply take him and everything he is in a single moment. Images of standing before him undressing him smoothly really turning him on. Feeling the nature of his piece as it rises in full notice extremely turned her on. In that thought her phone rings, it's him sounding delicious so, she could just eat him up. She wants to taste his lips, kiss his neck and every last part of him. She wants to be intertwined within him like so. The sound of his voice immensely turns her on. His vocal as he speaks so precise as his day was very long as hers. He wants her the same but he's so damn proper in looking after her in saying you need your rest. All she can think is too hell fuck with my rest I need to be played up in your sex right now, yes boo that's what I need.

He shows and it's on now. From the welcoming at the door to the bedroom floor clothes are strawed about. Starting with his T, it's the first to go, next being her black very slinky nightie. He swoops her up into his being kissing her so very strong. She's kissing him back moaning and such she wants every piece and inch of him. Laying her on the bed she giggles I want you deep daddy, I need you deep as she unbuckles his belt slowly pulling his jeans down before him. Noticing she has no panties on he chuckles humm you ready for this meat. Oh yea baby I'm ready alright for you to feed me making me complete.

Tasting the vodka on his lips she knew it was about to be on. Feeling his nature as he brushed up against her touching her very strong. He was hard as a rock just as she liked as he begins to enter her. In that moment she whispers wait baby give me the honor of putting him right where she wants him. Entering her she's taken to that place of far away. Nothing else mattered nothing more existed in that moment of pleasure. She's taking him as fast as he can give it to her moans of excitements he knows. The knowing that he's about to give her everything she needed from when she answered hello. Kissing her neck down to her nipples and everywhere below sent her into a state of eroticism. She's scratching his back, clawing his arms, begging please yes give me more. Looking into her face as her eyes were closed he whispers baby look at me. Opening her eyes to his seductive sights made her lose it even more.

Is this how you want it, just like this as he's driving in and out, back and forth, fast then oh my very slow. She blurts ah yes baby yes you know just how mommy needs it. He's putting in work like only he does making her lose her everlasting mind. She can't think or even speak in that instance for she had completely been taken. He's making love to her and fucking her at the very same time. She's moaning ahh more fuck me more as she finds the words to speak. He shushes her saying yeah baby just as you wish. With one steady stroke just right she erupts like an overflowing volcano. Losing all control of all motor skills she is as if broken. In that moment seeing he'd really rocked her world turned him deeply on. Few more strokes he shot like a rocket so nice thick and very much hot. Hot like it had been boiling awaiting for her to put it on simmer. As she did.

Laying there bare in their a natural beings. Both so comfortable and set free within one another. Kissing her passionately as she to him they both are therefore at peace.

Embraced against and laced within they in the write a vivid fantasy are there by complete

The Aphrodisiac

She awakens from a dream of him to find him at her doorstep. Knock knock knock. Mind you this vivid fantasy was one like no other in a reality sense. To roll over looking at phone in notice of twenty missed calls same in messages received, she wonders oh my! My,My,My.

Distraught like, she let's him into her domain with looks of confusion and curiosity lying in her eyes. Seeing in fact sensing the discombobulation on her person he enters her personal space with a lengthy embrace in talks of how much he had been awaiting to see her. Confused she replied "well, is everything ok". In a response of "yes baby, oh yea I'm just fine". Even better so now.

Alike her fantasy vision she was just awaken from he took her into him just as much as. Taking his gentle hands in placement to her face he pulls her close landing a kiss on her forehead then morning lips. Kissing him she's taken by notice of his wants, his needs to be within her aware she wanted as much. Passion, fire, and oyea much desire in the passionate lascivious kisses they each share. Steamy embrace from him to her she's taken.

Wrapping his muscular arms around her waist he lifts her up onto him in stronger kisses declaring his want and need to just simply have her right then in that moment. Carrying her to the bedroom where he lays her ever so delicately on her place of sleep. Sweet tender pecks to her lobes, neck, and beyond had her in an erotic state of mental. Feeling every bit of what he was partaking of her she submitted much so obliging.

Taking his hands lifting her thighs as he plants juicy wet kisses before every sector of her being, she quivers and shakes. She's consumed by the heat from his tender kisses to her yoni that makes her very weak, she can't even speak. Lifting herself to see him in noticing, strong desire to watch him while he's stirring her pot. In doing he arises fully aroused and ready to enter his place of warmth between her thighs. With one swift insertion her body shifts. He goes in with such fullness she's completely taken. With each stroke he bore to her she's in much more deeper. Stroke, then kiss, the heat from her body was that of an inferno. He lit her universe afire in so much desire. Placing his hands around her neck gently as he gave her every enticing inch of him. The clutch to her hands as he embraced them squeezing from so much pleasure. Whispers of benevolence and needs of each, getting the release was at that point complete.

Gentle kisses to her body and sincerity that she's ok. He kisses her lips slipping in his tongue to taste. So much passion in this kiss had her wanting some more.

In that very second she thought and then spoke "oh my, now which of us is the aphrodisiac".

Quote:
When time and space are quiet...you will Always,
ALWAYS find me deep very deep in my poetic thoughts.
Meka©

Loving Me

In her one would see what only she allows you to see.
To see what's in their behind what's deep as
far as the naked eye of she.

Love, compassion, and empathy she possess
as well as inspiration, motivation, by determination.
A divine influence directly and immediately exerted
upon her mind and soul. A force influencing by causing
her to do what she sets her mind upon. Through a quality
which makes you continue trying to do by achievement
something once quite difficult.

To awaken knowing she to be apart of a selected of
chosen has opened her to all which surrounds her.
She see's herself as a survivor. Having coped very
well in difficulties meant to destroy her mental had
she allowed . Now embracing her refined purpose
and placement in her world.

Wanting to simply make a difference to others dealing
with setbacks and current situations thinking there is
no way out. Feeling stuck as though there's no tomorrow

giving you no hope. Feelings of being alone in everything as if no one else can even understand. At some point she awoken seeing things completely different. With a whole new outlook on her life. As far as her eyes let her see. She packed her bags leaving that life and entering a new so to speak. Full of poetical and intellectual thoughts, aspirations, hopes and dreams. Seeing each and every one in true form as they have and will become.

Remembering a time before at times when she didn't love herself as much. Makes her stronger in knowing she never wants to go back to that awful dark place within. A Place of hiding which she did very well. Not knowing that the beauty that lies deep was something the special did see. Here she stands the woman she is.

Beautiful, chocolate brown eyed sister. She's simply she. Perfect not me, that's something one will never hear me speak. A quality I simply do not possess. Here I stand in complete awe of simply loving me.

Quote
In our everyday life's lessons we partake a divine path to leadership, encouragement, & ownership. In doing so we are the living proof that with an open mind we each do have a open heart
Meka

Act2(Like The Very 1st Time)

He says do you want a piece metaphorically meaning come get your stick. Coming into him was like a breath of fresh air. His touch when he touches me makes me vibrate sensations my body has long awaited. Imagining his kisses to my frontal lobe down to my breast and umm of beyond has my hormones full blown for want, lust, and longing to feel the thrust of his strong very long chocolate hard on.

Thoughts to simply fuck this man to the month of May has me turned all the way on.

Taking his hands placing them within and all around my very natural hungry for more sexuality. His palms as they squeeze my much firm breast sends me to an euphoric place. Destination in Excitement and great happiness making me intoxicating love drunk. His lips so tender as he plants them up to mine, taste of spearmint as our tongues speak their language upon meeting. His kisses to my ear gives me butterflies, an erotic very sensual yet sensitive and tender emotion encounters me. One of want and more want.

The touch of his fingers as he runs them up and down my spine, makes me feel sexy as pure sexiness consumes me my alter ego steps in to play. If he was edible I just may have eaten him up like a afternoon snack.

Making his way all the way down in refined search for my other set of lips makes me weak at the knees. Getting there sends me on a sensational high to the farthest place of never returning.

His lips inside my lips has me clawing at the sheets beneath me moans for more. Taking my hands in placement to the top of his head pushing him in to feast me more like his mid day snack, has my juices a flowing like a river that was once dry. He has my toes curled in a way they are locked waiting for my bust to merely relax.

Mental breakthroughs and combustion. Mindgasms and orgasmic out flows in orgasms. Oohs and ahhs and such. Our bodies are intertwined becoming one. Legs merged together arms in lock of each others , sweat dripping, hot steamy passionate benevolence fucking making has me sprung like the very first time.

I Surrender

Giving into any and all
doubts hereby relinquishing
my body to your gathering.
Shh, baby no worries.
This here is all yours.
Touch me.
Tease me.
Gather me.
Closely as you open
this novel of romance within
turning my pages.
My mission is to simply
Intrigue you.
Deeply.
The journey's within me,
longing for your adventure in locating me.
In, and throughout, my essential
being. There is where
you will find me.
In all ways those in which you've
been needing.
In your lengthy pursuing
of me.
Taking my minds mental to destinations from your
persuasions unknown.
Faraway places only we shall
go.
Those in being of stimulation.
My plans are to in all ways

take your mind. By many ways
of taking my time.
In essentially penetrating
you.
As if marinating you in
saturation of all of me.

My wanting you, all of you.
Is In-fact found in you
wanting me,
yes all of thee.
I know you see.
We will be.
Allow in letting me take you Deeply.
Slowly.
Heavily.
Emotionally
Baby, I breath you mentally.
Within me, all about me.
Take me inside you,
In the knowing.
I won't break you.
Say no words baby, I was made for you.
Handsome one, you were
created in specifics just
for me.

Drink me down like your fine
glass of wine. Embracing my
taste upon your tongue.
Take your time in the sampling.

Making sure that you key out the
main ingredients.
Precisely.
Accurately.
In my entirety.
As you enjoy the delicacy of
me in your taste test.
The texture of my
moistness. The way it feels
as I melt within you.

Lay me out, like sheets of music.
To be moved by the lyrics I
play before you.
The graphic in my ballads, will
no doubt , reassuringly sooth
you.
No room for wonder, worry, or
thoughts of me not approving.
I in all ways completely trust
you.
In you inviting me to your laid
out playground.
To come join you for a
enjoyed playing in retiring.
I accept in allowing you
to lavishly take me.
My being in of
full blown submission.
With you.
Baby I hereby

completely Surrender.

Insight:
Inspirationally Inspired by Passion,Obsession,Creation, Expression,Vision,Daydreams, Emotions,Compulsion,& Beauty I am in all ways me. A Artist✦⋆☐ ☐ ☐

A Man Confused

She seemed dazed somewhat in a haze.
Contemplation's of simply going to him,
being within him.
You see he possessed a interesting way
in just mystically touching her, which took
her to a place of such distance.
Mystery yet charm, in so many ways even
strangers seldom wondered just what in-fact she simply
sees.

Behind those baby browns she sees mystic,a mystery.
He undoubtedly intrigues her in peeking her
inner interest. A fellow of such that's been hurt in of by
 his very own hands.
Playa playa oh back in the day. Present day not so much,
looking for stability inasmuch as.

Sights which touches her very core leaving her like a
drought in want for more.
His touch to her skin so gentle and meek
Strokes of embrace thread by thread she melts in mind too.
How he touches her soul to the last drop with whispers of
wants..
yea yearns, desires and needs for mores.
Imagines from yonder,
way back when she was more daring than
she'd ever indulge in this present day.

Soft kisses to the lips, passionate can't get enough embraces

all over.
Her neck to her ears, to her lips and oh yea
then more.
Grabbing her in doing so she pulls away
Pulling back in thought of drowning.
Differences in he to she, Shit she to be what is she thinking.
He is treading very softly much likely awaiting.
Simply awaiting their adventures rehashing journey.

Who was he which makes her feel as such.
Such ways of no explanation. Knowing completely in the knowing that every thing about this one she wants to the very core of herself within him. She simply tastes this man his energy, ambiance, his damn physic so to speak.
Very different ways. In him she sees something that leaves herself to wonder.

His ways of talk and that of such he's all hell
all over the place. He has her just as scatterbrained.
She can't even think, eat, or sleep.
She's at a lost, bamboozled so to speak, not understanding one bit what it means. To follow her gut when it speaks, it speaks in ways assuring her oh hell no this one is just confused.

The Melodies They Play

Beauty being skin deep is it's
truth when each speaks.
What lies beneath in each
as their benevolences truly unfolds.
She's his absolute radiant daylight
as he's unequivocally her knight in shining armor.
Undeniably having her back as she
in fact has his front.
Her king in their kingdom to his queen
of heart they each are quite the pair.

In her he has a life long companion,
as she in fact is a true connection,
to what seemingly feels like an opening
to his cores core.
His cohort from a social class of which
their very own.
Via his versatility in all his many ways.
He surely undoubtedly has her. He's in fact
her homey, her lover, and yes her very best friend.
Undeniable passions which run very deep
they two are what seems truly meant to be.

Rhythms in a song they both have a recurring
much natural flow.
Their hearts play lyrical sweet enchanting melodies
to each souls core.
They have each other like no other for he holds
her down mentally, physically, and oh yes spiritually

as she to him.
Never for seeing their love to change in their hearts
it will forever stay the same.
No worries of others for they are the only in each others
eyes.
They are their everything. Nothing's forward
about them when expressing how each feels.
Their prides are non existent.
It's them they each do need.
Forever and a day is how long they shall be,
flowing ballets of sweet in-depth lyrical melodies
in one another that they each
beautifully play.

Simply Be

He loves her because she's beautiful. Not in outside beauty only. He loves her for the beauty she possesses deep.
Her inner essential piece is what attracted him when they very first met. Essences beauty defined by refined in-depth lines leading to her very core. Leaving him intrigued in want for so much more.

A heart so purely pure he was magnificently drawn to her. Hungry damn like starving for just a little more. In quest for the more he certainly found a woman whose beauty shined further than his eyes could see. Past what his heart had ever touched.

In introduction he discovered he definitely unequivocally had to have her. For to live another day without her, his life would be hereby very incomplete.

The beauty that rested behind her eyes. Much far only he did see.
That of simple elegance, a radiant gem indeed. Such pure and honest heart really turned him on.
In not of sexual content. It was something mental which seeped from her intellect directly in accordance with his.

The ambiance from her being took him to this destination he had never been. He was in strong benevolence from the very beginning upon meeting her just by chance.

Where had she been all his deep

long days. In wonder if their meeting really were by odds chance. Her mind he'd fallen hard for her mental vibrations. Such intellectual intelligence she possessed. Rays from strays within sunshine which out poured throughout colorful rainbows. Their conversations were precise, much in lengthy chit chats. Speaks of tomorrow, what could be and would lead to conversations of distant pleasures left in her and their yesterdays. He certainly for she, as she indeed for him. Seemed they in fact were certainly what deemed to simply be.

A Masterpiece In Artwork

The artwork with his tool he did to her body was a
masterpiece.
You see he possessed a gift when with her the gift of being
a fine precise artisan with his hands, tongue and oh! oh my!
Practicing his trade of hands craft, craftsmanship
on her being not often enough yet just as much as
leaving her temporarily sat-is-fied.

Aphrodisiac as she, he was her food, drink, and drug
which stimulated her every sexual desire.
His roles played foreplay which brought heat from his loins
to her cores depth setting her soul afire as their physics
merged. Coming together, becoming one.
Uniting in of each.
The work he put into the fine tuning of her canvas
was one of an acquired such.
Getting, owning, and having her in completeness.
Defining in cultivating each and every line with precision
in-depth outlines.

In he she embodied a foreseen likeness in ways they both
never had gathered. He touched the very essence of her by
simply being. Strong benevolence in each as both
completes each sentences. He moved her world as she
shifted his so to speak. He was her day as she was his
night. They each were quite simply, lightly touched, very
finely brushed to in-fact with elegance be.
A exquisitely delicacy fitting just to be.
The Masterpiece In Artwork

made just for each.

Come Be With Me(Lost In The You and Me)

Come be with me under the night's light.
Yes this night.
Let's get taken by the gleam from the stars,
and the elegance within the moon.
Can't it be just you and me under the tree,
which sits underneath holding the branch,
which birthed from its sprouting roots.

In complete notice in of the way
in which the brisk of the breeze from the air
which we can not see
lightly brushing through
and around our physical beings.
Like vibrations waving in and about our entire reality..
And existence.
Lost in the entirety of this night as darkness continues its
fall. Come be with me.

Mystical visions within our thoughts and
euphoric suspenseful mental game.
In of our justly ways.
All alone simply lost.
Nowhere to be utterly found in
this you and me right here as we lay amid
those light lit stars, beneath that lively tree,
that oversees the awakening in the night from
which the moon shine so romantically bright.

That could be just you and me, if only you would let yourself be
Lost in the you and me.

The Refined One

When seeing him you will find that he's a man of many personalities.
Somewhat of a chameleon so to say.
Workaholic, Father, Husband, his boys Best friend.
Mr. Working friendly, family man.
Everyday duties from days into days out.
He's most occasions always always home by eight.

At the office or in the field you will find him working his positions duties, task, functions too.
With very great effort.
Serious-minded, earnest disposition, very trended in his thoughts. Focused.
He puts his sole attention and energy into his workmanship. A quality allowing him to deal with issues at hand in a determined and effective way. He has a capacity for exertion and endurance. Quite the hard working stud in fact.

Superhero in the sparkling sights of his young-lings.
In him they see strength, a quality and state of being physically strong. A solidity and toughness
He loves them with every fiber of his being and more.
They see his love when feeling his benevolence in their each and every day interactions.

He with stern help ensure home lessons are complete, chores are met, all the while conversing on how their days gone. Time consumed in playful occurrences are in the most always eventful episodes.

British speaking term the steward he is very much so the married man. Mister in his lovelies light brights. Feelings are strong and constant never fading in her. Attractions and affections he in doing profoundly expresses. Warm attachments within her are met. She's his beloved, darling a fondness and much devoutness to her oozes surrounding his spirited being.
Respect is mutual he purely loves every way and thing about her, her essence has him attached. Their copulation when embraced is always blissfully great. They are the perfect suitable mates.

A homies best friend he surely is. Much familiarity in the neighborhood. They shoot the breeze, laugh, cutup occasionally play some rounds or twos. They're boys, best friends, whom help and support one another. No hostilities between these comrades, a foe as in enemy , oh no. Their respects are many from absolution's in understandings, forgiveness in misunderstandings too. Which are seldom few.

In analyzing him out closely and very carefully. It is learned the nature and relationships, the essential parts of he have been examined finding he is in fact a Refined one.

Place Your Blame

I suppose it makes you feel better to call her out of her name, down grades in insults when conversing of her person. Do as you may, whatever you deem you need to try making your inner feel somewhat better.
The childhood term Stix and Stones may break my bones BUT words will never hurt me, really does apply.
Do as you must, in doing as you may , whatever helps you justify the many mistakes you made. The faults you still continue to adhere to this very day.

When peace within is made, there's truly no space for fault. It in fact is a tranquility and a state of quietness, you should really do some trying. A freedom within that leaves no room for war, which you apparently are still in dealings with.
 Your conflagration isn't with she it's indeed with self, and until you profoundly relent and part with it, you will remain still in the same place.
So you just go right ahead wallow In your childish games. Point your misdirected finger, place your silly blame. Whatever helps you sleep and not think about what really would've been. I mean come on isn't that really what your problem is.

Seldom wonders, and concerns of your physical well being, has slowly with time, faded far away.
Left now with pity which in its self is for a matter of fact quite damn despicable. There comes a time when one must really do some reevaluating, and reflecting upon self. Fore

it in-deed would show that you have a lot of cultivating to do. But whatever makes you feel well in taking the weakness from yourself.
In fully rehabilitating one will change. In seeing things in a completely different light. There would definitely be no room left for your self inflicted damn shame. Which in-fact is exactly what you feel. Yes its what you've deemed heavy upon yourself. You see the difference between you and she is that she really did take the time in doing some self reflect. Taking ownership in her parts in why the relationship after time finally desolated. In reflections, evaluating, and deep rooted self improvements brought about a strength in her that you can never break. So go ahead with your wallowing, your drinking yourself to a pope, your pathetic lies in insults, if that's what really helps.

You see what you don't see is that with time brought some growth. She will not wallow in your disgrace and your unfounded growth. All your "baby I'm sorry", "I will never do it again," even your "oh baby I will get the help I need". The very many "baby your the only friend I got", oh and my favorite one of all like your mind really slipped. "Baby I just really do not even remember."
Again if that's what makes you feel better in taking the shame from yourself,
You go right ahead because shame doesn't reside here.

The One Her Heart Belonged To

Their she lay very sweetly
meek in just of simply being.
Occasional occurrence in thoughts of he seeping
in entrance to her draw-ed out mental capacities.
Should she or shouldn't she is what she plays over back and
forth in ponder at the very notion. Phone calls and text
messages off and on throughout the day,
in showing she's value to daring
being.

Baits and declares in wants on
what if's peeks her interest of
the such possibilities. Could
it be this he was indeed weighing
In on her cerebral strong mental.
He's making her weak is how
she plays of it in making excuses
trying to in fact within herself.
Fear, and disbelief in the knowing
that yes this is really happening.
He's tripped over hard in infatuations of her and she in
squandering adheres the same.
Or is it justly justified in much of being really just that.

Reluctant by such foolishness of extravagant love and
admiration
she really doesn't want to own it.
In holding by possessing it would
leave her open to embracing

what felt like excruciating
aches from hurt.
If things not work out in being
what they seem to be.

She needed to make dealings
with what she was feelings. She
was human in her wants, desires,
needs, and hungers. But could
this he informed by knowing
in-fact handle her. The burning
question she didn't want to carry
was could she take on him.
All he was offering within his ways of how he'd just simply
be.

To be within him was as inhaling a long awaited breath
after coming up from water.
He mysteriously by surprise with in depth elaborated tender
converses took her breath away. With hello sweethearts,
how was your day.
All day throughout her day each
and every which occurred.
In trying to keep him at arms
length she had fondly started
to have strong desires.

Finding herself craving by missing his presence
somewhat stirs her essential core. In friendly
mere romantic text she expresses admitting
she in-fact does long for him after his words of

expression met up with her first. Declarations of her being
quite the woman of what he felt to be exquisite and good.
For as long as he's known her he expresses he's seen this
ambiance which she possess. Surely making her simply
melt fore she disbelieved he could even see that far.
Not of absolute certainty still she
expresses a deep heartfelt thank
you. In wonder amazed somewhat dazed definitely
speechless she seemingly ponders.
Is he the one in which her beating vessel
shall reside in with his mysteriously belonging.

A Ball Of An Evening

Pulling out no stops
she was in for the
finest surprise.
A magical night just
them two at what seemed
to be, in likeness of a
cathedral hall. Filled
with mystery and delight
made her essence shine
with seemingly natural beauty.
Which intrinsically seeped in
pour outs, soft twinkles very
bright like, in loveliness
through her eyes.

He had a special way of
making her feel as though
she was the only woman
that subsist in his world.
Having actual being.
With such elegance and
sophistication he casually
wine and dined her on non-special
occasions especially.
In chance and opportunity.

She possessed a classy,
very independent enchanting
way about her that really

drew him in.
Intrigued indeed.
Everything she embodied as a
person made him want; having
to embark within through
out every part of her, even more.

They danced and swayed listening to
exquisitely delicate ballads of jazz.
In stand off taken by
sweet blissful melodies,
which played throughout their
very spirits. Chit
chats back and forth in
enjoyment of one another
as they chilled fully in romantic refined
worldly-wise conversations, in perfect
posture.

The attractions among them
was Mental, for their minds
at times were unresponsive from
emotional and intellectual
vibrations. Spiritually having similarities
in values, ideas, and beliefs. Cosmically,
in their mindset they were the only two which
existed. Physically, they were hot.
In ways their bodies touched.

The lighting in the hall gleamed
so dawned bright outlining with

precise divinely lines of each
very being in every smooth move.
Temperature in the space in which they were.
To be perfect to the moments being shared.
Placing and keeping them in comfort zone
mode.
As their evenings progressed.
The night was fairly coming
to an end.
Both deciding upon a
nightcap with their finest bottle
of champagne. Underneath the very moon
that circled their earth shining in the night by
reflecting light from their sun. Lighting up their
points of light which are often called stars.
White Satin table cloth which
overlaid the table so
elegantly. Boutique styled crystalline glasses.
One in which a formal setting.
Not stopping at the detailed, tasteful only special
occasions, silver in flatware. Light lit lanterns
overseeing the friendly tree which seemingly lit up
the dark nights sky.
All of the in said darkness falls was quietly
sealed in much detail.
To be in-fact of what they both
shared.
A very beautiful
Ball Of An Evening.

Destined.... Meant To Be

In and throughout every part of astrology
from the beginning to the end
you will meet one person who is
distinctive to any other.
You could converse with this
person for hours at any particular
time on any given day as you may,
and never get bored.
You could share with them things
and they'd never referee you.
Not at anytime forming opinions of your person
after careful thought.

This person is your soul mate, your
best friend. Better than all others
in value and respect. Most skillful, talented
and successful. Most appropriate, useful
and helpful. In completely understanding
you, becoming in being your counterpart.
A one in which is remarkably the
same. Not different. Exact in fact.
Not changed.
A distinguish-ably identical coequal,
He's ably recognized as different.
You see and hear him clearly.
Unchanging, Constant, Immutable one
whose heart completely parallels in with
yours. Extending in the same direction,
 everywhere equidistant.

Equidistantly equal.

The same in degree, rank, and said quality.
Identical, Equivalent, Impartial.
Physical, mental, and emotional traits
are in of exact alignment.
The proper positioning in with your person
your being.
They are in fact your ideal one.
Unequivocally in ideology,
you are destined...meant to be.

A Familiar Piece

Excuse me for being so forward but I just have to have you
and everything you possess.
You see baby I've been feenin for your chocolate dick since
our last encounter.
When thoughts of you creep into my stirred up mental
throwing it on the back burner I just can't do any longer.
I need and want some of your good protein and I'm looking
for you to administer some oh hell all of that
Sweet
Strong
Very long
Nutrition hard on stick that I've been longing.

Baby when I turn the pages in my mental play I press
rewind then
forward over and over. The things
you do to and with me sends me to a euphoric place.
Thoughts of your hands caressing my fullness sends me to
a level of no return. Your tender kisses to my frontal lobe
making your way to my breast
Making my titties stand at attention from so much
submission. And oh my yes down a little further.
The way you grab my ass like so, as I ride you for the
overhaul long drive.
Making me cum multiples over and over for what seems
like hours and hours.

No sir not a minute man, that you are not which damn that
really turns me on. The way you take your time making

quite sure that all of my needs are surely met. Taunting me with "Does that feel good",
"Do you like it like that",
knowing very damn well I'm addicted to the things that your dick do. The way you express yourself when I'm administering my foreplay really really turns me on. Making me enjoy taking you within and between my luscious lips with definition each and every damn time.
Your magic stick be at grown
man attention too just the way I extremely like.
Hell who am I kidding we both very well know fuck I LOVE the shit your dick do.
When you are so precisely feeding me until I am very full.

Come see me baby, I'm quite malnutrition-ed fore it has been a very long while. I'm so selective in who I lay with, I can't be calling any other nigga. It's you baby I've been daydreaming about and that's consuming every bit of my nightly visions. I'm hungry for the familiar, in it being you.
Come boo boo and make my body rock,
Quake,
And shake.
Don't be coy,
Come and get me.
Taking me anyway you want me.
In this bed, on our spread I'm craving a familiar piece.

Satisfying The Hunger

In one single moment how can it be possible that he could come
onto me making me feel
sensations of ecstasy in that
having been long awaited.
Moving a mountain in that of
being me, causing my soul to
leave my earthly possession.
To stir and gather around to
only re-enter me passionately.
Deeply.
Putting me in a state of mental eroticism.
Taking these vibrations of being movement all about with patience.
As they each take a hold of
me.
Grasping me
Feeling me
Fucking me by
Loving me
Lightly finger fucking my
essences purity.
Purifying me.
It is he that gives my entire
 being these ageism that takes
me to places in which I've never
in my entire earthly existence ever gathered.

He knows exactly where to touch

me deep. Which makes my core
seep.
Weep.
Cry.
From deprivation. The want,
the need. Of being simply had.
The places that makes
me unable to speak. Leaving in having me breathtakingly
consumed by all arrays, and
taken by and in all which he offers
all of me.
His soft kept hands to my
lower back makes me embrace
what feels like earth moving quakes that in self I only
acknowledge in partaking.
As I take from within and
all about, feeling the head
of his dick as it is a masterpiece
as I feel it in-depth vibrating my
insides,
swelling in all the places
in which it dwells
causing my body
to have these uncontrollable
shakes in sensations
Succumbed by nothing more
than consumption as he makes
love by passionately fucking
me to my essential.

Knowing very well he himself

feels the movement.
The shakes, and the breaks.
Which makes my heart
palpitate with yearns from
aggression.
The mental Orgasms in which
my body takes.
Damn near breaking,
for all of him to see.
In all of my vulnerabilities.

Touching me in embracing
to the back of my thighs, underneath my ass pushing
me so lovingly in so much further
in deepness as I can possibly
go. Filling me up as if my bodies
this empty tank in needing of
a refueling in which he's much obliged in giving being his dick
is all that's needed.
Hearing me moan in
delightful from being so
full with his thickness from
wall to wall, feeling him inch
by yummy delicious inch.
As he administers me his swift
abrupt dicktation.
He makes my mouth water
from the thirst to simply
drink from his essence of
being.

Quenching my thirsty thirst.

I eat him up emptying myself
all upon him as he strokes me,
my pussy, and my mental for so much
more.
Wholeheartedly in giving I
give relinquishing every single
piece of me.
Giving him my all.
I am that of a vessel
Seemingly hollow.
Only he can do me such a way,
in which I lose all touch of
reality, completely lost in
every bit of what he's giving
in offering.
He knows exactly what my body
needs and doesn't mind giving
when the moment in time
arises.
Leaving me so damn gooey,
completely satisfied and very
much in nourished
 in all of my sluggishness
from the explosion that he
sends from what's inside pouring to the outside as I cum
with
power.
Completely aroused.
Until the next encounter.

In my being of giving him
all that I am and all that
I have to give he in
all ways of completion
Satisfies My Craving Of
Hunger.

She Was Took

Taking her within his web of love and so much heat.
He made her soaking wet.
Cuffing his hands between her thighs just to get a sample of the way her heat felt turned him massively on.
Quick like he grabs her in a embrace, seemingly knocking her off her feet as she is completely succumbed
within him,
beneath him,
all about him.
She had to trust him.
As she did.
He could have in doing what ever he deemed necessary in rocking her body hard.
He was a pro. At doing just that.
It was his civic duty to do those things which made her addicted to what his dick did.
Swift dicktation strokes
fast,
steady,
slow,
round and round
oh my she was assured to blow.
From so much flow.
He made her go.
Over and over, in
time and time a "fucking" gain.
She as he was Hooked!
He was taken by the way her body shook.
As she was took.

It Was A Blow"RAW"

Her mind was in a daze. Somewhat of a haze. Thoughts, wants needs, desires anything and everything came to mind. In times like these she needed a good ole fashion lashing. A ultimate fucking her toy just couldn't handle. To be completely taken into someones cocoon. Strong yearn to be taken in full blown detail. Undressing her slowly in touch of every line within her. Slow tender kisses to her ear down to her neck and um yea her breast too. Sucking her nipples nice and slow and all around. Gentle sucks and tongue flicks making her slap damn fucked up crazy. Slowly work your way down to her belly doing your thing with the button. Having her intoxicating fucked drunk awaiting your strong arrival. The closer you get to her vulva you see it just in purr. Juicy nice and wet. Heat felt from near. Ready and wanting, waiting your insertion. You feel her begging for it as if a damn crack feened crackhead. Her want has her in so deep so she can't control a thought or even move. Upon you entering her so gentle nice then hard. She squeak out an out pour of oh yes baby fuck me more. The arch of her back is up her head tilted so far back. She's moaning so damn uncontrollable baby give me it all. Tears a flow she's in it to win it she wants your extended flow. Thick rich milky white shit gushing beneath her baby it was a blow.

You Left Without Saying Goodbye

You were here one day and then you were gone.
Leaving imprints of your being all around hear
and there.
Your smell still among-st in every place near and far.
To stand in normal daily activities roundabout
here and their.
Echos of your voice I like to imagine I sometimes
really would like to hear.
In wonder of how your vocals would be.
Low tone or baritone I often squander in the wonder.

Your personality I often find myself in curiosity of oh
how you would be in
Interacting.
Would you still have that big bright smile in which you
glowed having possession
In just the six months of age.
With what seemed like shining bright like eyes.
Which were in-fact one of
 the very light in mine.

How would you look in-fact.
Still to having those chubby cheeks.
In wonder I often marvel at this notion as to what
you as a person would be like in this day in time.
Would you be so full of life, determination with
eagerness in possession.
What in-fact would your aspirations be.
Your hopes, dreams and admiration's.

Would you be the go getter.
All you put your being into leaving the world
in your fingertips.
These are things I hoped for you in wishes
which I silently whispered in prayers.
Kissing you on your forehead,
with my index finger holding
yours.
These were my hopes, dreams
and aspirations, I lovingly,
wholeheartedly wanted for
you, my precious one.
On that of the day I birthed you.

Knowing now with age and growth
that you did in-fact tell momma goodbye.
In the way I embraced you,
patiently back and forth I rocked.
Sweet Lullabies; calming, quieting,
and soothing as I patiently
sang to you while you laid
their in your piece within
my arms.
I was given such
 a great honor In which I now do see.
The pleasured privilege
of embracing you as you
went off into your deep sleep
in piece...........

                 For ✦ ▫ ▩ ▫ "Joshua"✦ ▫ ▩ ▫ ▫

Stop And Pose

You see her and you are in
awe of her radiant glow.
She possesses a beauty
which is exquisitely natural.
Fabulously lovely their she
stands diva of a goddess.
The men all flock in want of
nothing more. Just to be near her
adhering presence.

African American beauty. Yes
that is what she is in all of
her many ways. She's versatile
quite factual, very flexible in
her proper being. A variable
queen yes indeed. Embracing
variables with such ease as she
takes on one thing ah yes and
another.

Look at her in amazement,
bewildered, by astonishment
she is quite the eye-opener
as you should indeed see.
She's ravishingly breath-taking.
Chocolate Nubian knockout.
Seemingly to be an enchantress
she who uses spells or magic. A
sorceress. Oh no that she's not.

She inherits a loveliness, a
quality in her which gives pleasure to her senses and
pleasurable delights to
the naked eye. Which
pleasurably exalts the mind and
spirit of all those she encounter.

Her psyche is that of a force
within her beloved in giving her
life, energy, and yes in-fact power.
Her inner quality which out-pours
through her outer.
She is a queen unequivocally of strength, courage, and
wisdom. Fore she is the wisest in her group.

Ancestors In which she comes from a long line of.
She is a gentle soul. A fine, divine, gem piece.
Her person's deeply felt
moral and emotional nature.
Her attractiveness is in-deed a art.
She is enchantingly gorgeous in her unsightliness.
To not see her laced in beauty
with assurance and certainty
makes you blind.

The feathers she exhibit with pride, elegantly floral from
above
her mighty wise one strongly represents that in which she
stands for. Her particular state said tribe even.
Her people those which she
stands for.

Her armor right down to her earrings is a definite representation of said power and uniqueness....Their she stands, hear she is, for all to see. Presented to you in her essential ebony glow. Stand Stop And Pose

Rapture

Sliding off her panties he was
on fire he simply had to have
her. Touching her softly with
gentle touches he wanted every
Inch of her.
She wanted him too for she was
starving for his flaming hot
hard-on. She wanted him to
touch her places she knew
only he could catch. Taking
his hands in placement cuffing
by embrace to her firm
voluptuous ass.
That a surely turned her all the
way on as if she had been
boiling over a very hot stove.
His pot of honey which in him he
was of absolution.

She had been dreaming of him
in all of her nightly visions
for two very long months and
three drawn out days now since
their last encounter. It had been
entirely too damn long.
She wanted to absolutely
ravishingly rape every sector and
enticing inch of him.
She ran that over and over

throughout her mental as she
allowed him the honor and
privilege to take her there.
She was horny as hell
and wasn't afraid of making him
aware.
Fore he was her man and it
was his duty to see that her
needs were no doubt met.
She jumped before him
causing him to take possession
of her exposed very whole being.
Naked before him as he examined
each and every line she with stood
so daring bare.

He laid her down kissing her softly
from head to toe. Starting
at her forehead making his way
all the way down to her steaming
honey pot. Her essence core
burned from yearns as his
loins ached to be inside of her.
The fire they made was so damn hot they
both burned like flamed
Chard coal.
You see they were very hot.

She missed every piece of him
she softly whispered before him
as he lovingly took her.

As she knew he would he
skillfully took her to that place
of no return.
Such a beautiful out pour of
love and endurance is what they
indeed shared.
Their emotions got the best
of them as they both were
consumed within their romantic
pleasure.

He was her lollipop, as she was his cherries.
They both were simply good to the very last drop.
The moment in the night with
stood the time in which they
had longed for one another.
Through intimate in dept phone
conversations while he was away.
In those very hours they had
just shared an exotic very erotic
drawn out fantasy.
In awe of each other
they were in
complete rapture.

A Good Night's Sleep

For as long as she could remember
when searching her
main framed
mental
she wasn't able to gather when
it was last that she slept in
completeness.
Deep comprehensive wholeness.
With another individual.
That being told a mind strong,
bonafied quite studly man.

She had longed for so long
she began to believe she no
longer knew what it in-fact
felt like to simply be laced
in an embrace of
meaningful,
in-depth,
sensual,
very
passionate,
peaceful escape.
Surely aware, patience is
essentially relevant in this
said peace of being.
She awaits it.

Longing,

Needing,
Wanting,
in the waiting gives her a
solace in the knowing that
she will indeed capture this
feeling.
It will in all actuality
beautifully take her by ways
of consumption upon
occurring. There by
taking of completion,
a full in-depth by length
a hold of her being
like a summers
breeze in the
heat
of
a very
hot day.
She will with no
uncertainty
In assurance
dutifully
 wait
just for that.
A Good Nights
Sleep

Destiny Awaits (Or Doesn't)

You know when you know who
it is that you are destined to
be with. From the very moment
their presence met up with
yours. The chanced encounter
of simply meeting. Upon meeting
you just unequivocally knew.
This here is the person,
that one other that makes your
heart skip beats.
Makes your insides flutter with
what we call butterflies.
From the anticipation in want.
Which intensifies whenever
there presence is near.

Communication with them is
easy at most. Unforced.
Any and every-thing from
sun up to sun down you two
do and can express.
A mutual respect in two beings
is what exist. Life's challenges
and ways. Happy moments
even sad ones too. You find
yourself longing to indeed share
with them.
In their arms is where
you feel you belong.

Secrets most tender ones too.
No-one else however in them
you indeed very well speak.
Fore you know in them no
judgments are made or will
ever be done.
You supply each other with
a gentle,loving,nurturing solace.
A quietness, offering a stillness.
You are peaceful within each
others space.

Seeing each other at times are
painful. Due to the strong
in-depth feelings of benevolence.
In each for one another you in-fact
do possess. Although a welcoming
by each is strongly with fondness,
greeted upon meeting after a
period of time. Your embraces
are as by being engulfed.
Thereby taken in a rapture way.
Of intense, pleasure, and so much
joy. You are thereby consumed in-fact.
You simply make each other better.
Your ambitions line right up
with their aims.
You with no doubt and uncertainties wish
them well.
In any and everything
they profoundly aspire.

A strong, deep nocturnal love.
Which also occurs in coincidence
throughout the day.
A attachment so dear that if the
two should not simply be. They wish the
 other the complete and utter best.

Relinquishing Her Panties

In a single moment he entered the room within her thighs
swiftly. Abruptly. Waking up sensations long awaited.
Her doors wide open for him to simply come right in as she
welcomed him upon driving to their destination.
Along the ride she took him to places he had never
gathered and if he did he wasn't letting on. Due to the
mental mind blown way she had his cerberal seeping.
Seemingly weeping, shit drooling so to say. Squeezing
giving him more. Toes curled, hair pulling, ass slapping,
jaw dropping hot sensual sex.
He in all ways had been taken.

His mental gasket had been blown and all the fluid he had
in holding had been what seemed to be evaporated.
Gone
Kaput.
The fuel it took for him to get to the destination being her
level had somehow ran out. He was mind boggled as to
how on earth this woman could make him nut up from the
sun up. A way he hadn't ever shot. She smiled from
enjoyment in knowing she conquered what she had set out
on a mission to accomplish in the adventure of blowing his

mind. He couldn't escape. As it was it was taking all he had to simply call out her name. In saying baby, oh my please. Her curiosity had been peeked as she had been pondering over the idea for sometime now of how she was going to show him, he being the one stuck on teaching her somethings or two. Huh! She had just taught him by showing him all the woman she was when it came to sexually satisfying her man.

She was satisfied now. Her task had been done and was complete. As she leans over in asking him, baby, you ok? His reply, Damn baby

Smacking his ass she responds, Now pick your jaw up you just got taken.

As she relinquished in giving him her pink panties.

P.S. I Love You

Since the making of man
and that of woman it has
been known.
The fundamental affections
that's partaken through
fond
giving and
taken ways delivers a said
endurance.
A very natural emotion that's
known to in ways by
consumption, take over
every
ounce and
piece of you.
Dissecting you bit by bit
till all you are is a mirroring
image of the other.

Out pours of
intense,
blistering,
excruciating by fear.
In-depth,
comprehensive,
panoramic, benevolence.
In taking this said
abundant from joy,
heart wrenching

roller coaster ride
all that's left for you
to do is
hold your composure.
You
are
taken.
Grasped and captive by ways
of movement in being carried
to places you never gathered
existed less known perceived.

Undergoing passive experiences
in all said senses of your natural
being. To lavishly
See
Smell
Taste and simply feel by touches
to your deep
Essence core.
Seemingly fingertip-ed.
All of which are indeed
accomplished
in-fact
Consummated.
Thereby perfected in it's
completion.
It's a very beautiful thing.
In which is known of taken
one by surprise.

As of writing
a lengthy novel of all the ways
you simply enjoy and care
just to leave the best part for
last.
With an enchantingly
elegant
beautiful and
sentimentally
sweet
P.S. I Love You

Could've Been

Did he know what he was doing when he kissed her so ever
gently.
The closed door he opened releasing what had been
hidden.
Deep and far within.
Did he know the lasting Impression he would
severely imprint among
her entire soul,
in being just simply near his wholesome presence.
In the way he gentle touched
her face lifting it so, aligning
to meet up with his.

Setting her very existence to
a fast slow motion.
Being near him scared her
like hell.
She shook.
She was took.
From the inside to her outside.
A fear within of
him being completely aware
that she wanted every bit of
what he was.
What if's and maybe if we'd
they both with intensity
did indeed play on constant
replay when images of
their past were in full length

there as rehashed.

 Did he know that she
would fall so madly in love
with just the thought of
waking up to him all in
with him. All which was
set into motion behind
that one intense,
earth moving,
in-depth
passionate laced kiss.
Which caused her body
to vibrate sensations she
never gathered existed.
He Initiated and
Implanted
by Administering on her much hungry tender lips.
Setting into motion an unseen
chain of events she hadn't
fathomed being apart of.

Covering by smothering her entire emotional being.
What if she had stayed with him way back then,
when she felt that running was better than a let down.
Oh if she could go back to
that way back place.
She would single out
in changing just only that one event.
Just to see what their future's really could've been.

In Check

We sat out tonight underneath the stars
in the back seat of his extended cab pickup.
Listening to Streetwise Jazz
a little bit of that Najee I might in-fact add.
Straight fit for a retiring we both
were laced in embrace
fancy like and shit.
The gentle smoothness of his skin as he
gently brushed his hands across my face.
The way he caressed the back of my neck
as he formally administered me a massage.
Made every strand of hair stand two
feet from deck.

The jazzy sounds set the mood so right.
As he moved in a little closer.
Turning me on being the perfect gentleman.
That blood rushing moment arrived where
our brown eyes met as if they'd met up
for the very first time.
Placing his hands cuffing my breast,
sent chills down my spine
and all up my racing chest.
Sending me to this distant mental place
deep within.
My body ached, feeling it shake from
malnutrition-ed hunger
so to say.
I was famished, fore I hadn't dined

in a very long time.
The absolution from my thoughts
of having him in the backseat of his
 extended cab pick-up.

Leather seats, cold to the touch as our
bodies met. Fogging up Windows
as though it was 50° below.
Being 80° much in-fact.
He made my soul burn from the fire he set,
setting my entire being to a blazing flame.
Sexy talking ways to me he spoke
as he slowly took me under causing me to
surrender in taking my time.
In our little adventure.

I straddle him ever so fondly.
Taking my hands and playing
with him gently. In tender, loving ways.
Placing him exactly where I wanted him to
make his grand entrance in appearing from a long while.
His hand placement was on point,
I wanted him to come in for
just a little more..

Hitching my dress up, touching me their.
Made me want him
so much more.
I'm on top deck now administering my play
so sophisticated like as he has me.
All the way in check.

You Can't Have Me

When searching for the words
to write. She successfully search
her heart in depth. Acquiring all
feelings,
emotions,
and tendencies.
A blah of a day in all of its said
occurrences in which affected
her mental deeply. Lost in her
mental mindgasmed thoughts,
she was sent on this inbound
dreadful journey.

Rain rain go away please come
back a later date, is what she
in alone a fear, embraced.
Watching the drops as they fell,
out her bedroom window.
As she tenderly in peace laid.
Dismayed.
Discouraged.
Alone.
Watching something on her
television screen in notice
that it in-fact was watching her.
Everything so quiet and peace
was still.
Should have been as of offering her
a tranquility.

A peace being still.

Wondering of days to come
those which in themselves
hadn't even happened yet.
Logically in pondering of
how to continue, in making
ends meet.
Determined in-fact of not going
down that gravel topped road.
Filled with bumps, curves,
lots and lots
of loose defining fine in of
precision rocks.
Remembering in the knowing
that her father God he had her in this.
All she had to do was call.
As she always did, just in
this day of dismay she was near
at lost.

In realization of where she was
heading. Her heart as if taking
life itself, spoke to her.
Saying.
Demanding.
Call him now.
Willing her by springing her
ass out of that funk, she was
suddenly on a different page of light.
One full of literature, deeply intriguing her way pass what

her mental seemingly
had gathered her.
The mind is a beautiful vessel
when maintained in a healthy
manner. By feeding, fueling,
and educating it. You must/
I must nurture it.

It would be so easy in just
to wallow in self inflicted pity
and her confined dismay.
The sun indeed will shine
today.
She knows by reassurance in assuring this.
By righteously in determining
so by deciding
 "No, not today".
"Satan, you can't have me".

In Making It Real(Daddy's Home)

It's early in the morning as she was just beginning to rise up out of bed. Her phone at once dings. A certain assigned ring which she's given to her booboo. Message reads hey baby are you woke, what are you doing.
Feeling a little devilish and freaky might I add. Her reply simply stated, hey boo I'm fine. Just done Playing while thinking of you. His wonder as he's fully aware in always knowing, although he still fixes his words to question. Oh, are you still in between our sheets right where I left you. As if answering his very own question he replies oh never mind, baby daddy's on his way.

Now in notice of her now mental state. She's seemingly enticed, ready as her insides began to crave so much more. She smiles rushing on out from beneath the covers for the shower to freshen up a little. As it was truthful she had just got done playing solely thinking of him and all the ways he moves her mentally,
physically,
emotionally so. Even though she had, she was nowhere near a complete
full length defining monumental orgasm to place on her shelf. Within herself. In the shower only Momentarily her mind begins to wonder. As the water from the drip hits over all areas of her bare sexy body. Gasping as the water hits her face
her mind begins to travel vividly
through her thoughts of all the ways he pleasures her. It had been so long felt like her visions were all she had in

holding on to, to remember in partaking she was really tripping being she'd just been within him last nights past. Fantasizing. Umm how he always takes me there. He umm yea "he".. He does such things that makes her body just cry. From being so deprived.

Mesmerized by her dark and lovely. She's tantalizing to his mind causing these chain reactions. She's completely aware of those things in which she does that makes him keep coming home for more. She's been told by he a million and one times oh my
baby you really put it down. If as in he "she knows how to definitely put him down each and every time. She gets great pleasure in feeding him when she herself is quite famished. Tasting him until he's thick and very long. Taking ownership of his chocolate thick masterful piece.

Her fantasies in the shower have somewhat got out of hand as her thoughts are all over the place as the sounds of the shower starts to fade away. She finds herself moaning not even touching herself as her visions have somehow taken rule. She loves the way she sounds the way he makes her sound. When remembering their night before episode, they're emotionally taking her their.
Embracing the drips as they lightly drop covering every sector of her nectar. She's on fire inside the shower. Mentally challenged unable to gather just what it is she jumped in for. She at once snaps out of it as her mind begins to come back from this such far away place. In lala land. As she hears Ding Dong.

The Doorbell rings..ooh wee yes daddy's made it home. Time to make it real.

His Kept Woman

On her throne is where you will find her.
She wears her crown of being
his very well.
With pride.
Power within which seeps out of her dutiful being
in ways only seen by those with vision.
Seeing what lies deep you know what creeps
beneath ones bare core. All the way down
to their essential glow.

It would take a very high wind to come through
and blow her away. Being though her presence
is one of enormous strength. Nothing in no one
can break her in the eyes of this man.
Her man.
Strong willed, determined in all said ways makes
her the chosen of, in, by strength one that she is.

To him she can do not wrong, fore her non doings
are those in basics. Anything and everything
within, about, and from her just being,
he willingly,
in lovingly,
by all means it seemingly moves him.
She motivates by encouragement. Administering
kind, encouraging words which has him taking
notice in the dime that she is.

She's a woman, lover, and his friend as well as

one to others.
His other half. In defining she's his counter-part.
A coequal. She's a mystery which intrigues
him, peeking his curiosity deeply.
When finding seeing in evaluating her with precision.
Unknowingly fallen in deep benevolence with her inner.
The parts never ever seen to any other of kind.
Untouched,
untamed,
unharmed from occurrences.
Though in-fact she is. From that which brought
her strength. In compassion from that which lies
very deep.
As if her spirit was aligned to meet right up with his.
He is in all ways and arrays in that of awe in being thereby
taken.
Taken about of whom she is.
That in who he see's her as.
His queen.

Enchanting beautiful smile which light up his nights sky,
eyes like crystals which sparkle of the brightest stars.
His shining one.
She's his butta love
His honey
His wonder woman
of a Goddess Gem.
His Kept Woman

Come Home

If she expressed to you
deeply. How much she
misses you. Your scent,
your being, every sweet
thing that seeps you.
It could never be enough
of expression for the way
she feels when her thoughts
of you consume each and
every breathtaking piece
of her.
It's mental
Physical
Emotional even.
Your presence she still feels
within her spirit.
Touching you,
You showing
her all those things in love.
In which made her heart
skip all those beats.
Two for each second
she spent with you.
Her earth broke like shatters
of glass that moment in time
when it stood steal.
Nothing in it made plain
sense.

Her heart breaks in places she
never knew existed.
Feelings for you
she never knew she could
gather.
Those which takes her breath
a thousand and one times.
She feels you when she sleeps,
when she tries to eat,
When she breaths.
Plagued with faded memories
which are still quite vivid.
She never told you.
You made love to her mind.
While stimulating her core.
Made it OK for her to feel sound.
Whole
Complete
It was you.
With you.
Just you.

As she sets sipping
her glass of wine
It helps when contemplating
through her elaborate mental
Seeping out-pours in overflowing
thoughts of you
Pouring out like water.
She fell in love with you more than
a time or two

Over and
over
and again.
Those times you'd sit up
for hours talking of
nothing at all.
Her homie.
Lover
Her best Friend.
The one that never made
her cry.
Always going that extra
mile.
In assuring she smiled.
That was you
It was you
It is you
As she searches for the
words to say.....
All she needs is you.
Her sun which shined
when it rained,
On a cloudy day
You were her month
of May
On a beautiful bright
day.

Slowing it down..
Baby I want you.....
I need you

I miss you
Baby,.....
It was you!
Come home

All That Of Being Me

She sat out tonight.
Watching the moonlight
All the way
As she'd say
Chilling on it.
She's all the way relaxed
within.
Not stressed out.
I'm saying
She real tight like
You know
Straight like that.
Her finest bottle of
wine she's complete
In it.
Like so.
Sweet beats in sounds
Listening to that jazz
play.
She's mellowed out
whole.
As she can simply
be.
Smooth
Carefree
Yea that's she.
Look for her you will
see. She's there deep
within her mode

set apart
in her mindfulness
and observations
recollecting
all her thoughts
Clarity in
Evaluating
Peeping things out
All noises cease to
exist
She's where she hears
herself be,
all of she.
Set free to be thee
In releasing her
Flo-etry in poetry
All that of being me.

Intellectually Inspired(Mind Traveling)

Have you ever been so
intrigued by a motivation
of something that leaves
you moved by inspiration.
To simply know more. All
their is to know.
To go on this feasting world
wind deeper than you have
ever allowed your mental
cerebral to go.
The place of higher learning
and sought out in-depth
knowledge.
The knowing which makes
you hungrier.

Educating yourself on said
topics in hand which makes
you unable to even focus on
any other as much until
you've satisfied that
craving.
The craving of knowledge.
It's emotionally stimulating.
Inspirational as well as motivational as it definitely
in all defined moments motivates
you in fullness.
Deeply.
It drives you,

pushes you,.
It becomes you.
Through
Ambitions
Aspirations and
Pretensions
A strong desire for advancement.
A particular goal and aim something that you a being
hopes to do or achieve
The desire to be successful,
even powerful,
The acquired desire to
do things and be active.
Things in which plagues
you from the want,
the hunger,
the determination in
the more.
The hidden powers.
The constant repeated
mental mindfulness and
observations.

Set apart from any other
being of that one.
Morning
Noon
Day and
Night
Any day in-fact.
Many responsibilities as

they may.
From the moment you
awake at the break of
any given day.
Morning wake-up,
casually into breakfast.
All the way to night fall,
when it's supper time.
Your mind is fully blown
into over-drive.
In all ways you've
made your day. But
where have you been in
that day.
Mentally
Emotionally
Psychologically
While you were working
your 9-5, during your
adventure in picking the
kids up, along the way of
getting home safe and
sound. Getting right into
doing your laundry, on
to the midst of cooking
dinner even.
Cleaning up the after-math.
Not to mention the areas of
time you spent conversing
in chit-chats.
All of which is In

essentially Being.

Just before you crash.
You ponder on those ways
and wonder.
Where were you.
Throughout the entire day.
In all of its Entirety.
Spiritually ,
Physically,
even emotionally.
Mentally..
I gather in wondering
if I'm simply mind
traveling.
Gathering everything I've
encountered in experiences throughout the over-all
day.
Which has left in leaving
imprints touching my soul in existence.
Bodies encountered, not even
of their physical bodies.
Again its emotional,
cosmic almost as if non existent. But they do exist because
your paths did
indeed cross.
In another time.
Another dimension.
Imprinted.
Strongly affected thereby influenced.
Affecting one in ways

unknown, to their simple
eye.
Although leaving them in a mental
space and place in this time.
Curious
Hungry in all ways of being
Intellectually
Inspired.

He Is Not Done With Me Yet

When looking in the mirror who does she see gazing back
looking at me.
A woman with determination. As
well as motivation.
Deeply inspired by the person shes become.
A woman whom is grateful for all she possesses.
Not in that of material things
as one would find in
gathering.
A caring heart is what she carries
Each and everyday as i in being.

What I love best of all, of my said
qualities in personalities. As you see do own a few.
Happy,
Grumpy,
Goofy,
Loving
Those are the selection of the few.
That I really do admire.
When happy one will see my smile, a charming one I like
to
quote it as.
Grumpy humm, not many see,
only those very dear to me. When
things somewhat don't seem to flow in the go of things.
Goofy! That I often very well am
on days when I just feel like such.
A complete and udder klutz.

I'm intelligent, caring, and very
smart. And some days I'm a complete mess.

What I enjoy most of all is that
I'm loving to my very core.
To look up love that is where I find me Myself
and I.
It is where my heart resides.
Deep in love with whomever it will that shall become.
Filled with passion, which makes
what feels like my heart skipping
beats.
That is what seeps
in,
threw,
and out of me.

I am not perfect as I as well have
this side, where things in people
really do piss me off.
Those occasions are when the
lion roars about in and out
of me.
Demanding to be heard, and
understood. That their are things
that I will not accept when coming
across and at me.
I demand respect, expecting at
all times. As I myself very well
give.
All these qualities I've inherited when my Father God made

in creating me. I know beyond any doubt I have room for more growth. These are which I do accept in knowing that he is not done with me yet

Games

One thing she must make
him understand in knowing
whom she is.
Playing is something she
just don't do.
In the greeting from said
meeting, one will acquire
such said knowledge.
Dipping
And
Dappling.
The hitting it
just to quit it
Isn't a thing of her in being.
The real, she's the
realest.
The truth, yea if it's you.

Question is, can you bring
it.
It being all she's offering.
One on one.
The commitment.
Loyalty, are you loyal.
Her plans can be in,
around,
with and
of being for you.
Seek her completely out.

All of her giving ways.
Listen with completeness
for who she really is.
Just make sure Man,
That you can with all certainty
definitely give it.
In your bringing.
No if's
Ands, or
Maybe's
Before she makes any
plans of being with you.

You will never have to question,
in worry.
Wonder, or dismay.
In not knowing
As with she, she will inform
you in her being.
In the very beginning.
Findings in her givings
are not to be just your
lover.
She's bringing a very
best friend.
A companion if that's what
your wanting.
She will not just settle
for any ole bull shit
Not her,
that you will

find.
See it clear,
See it as it is.
She's not this uptight,
in simple chick.
In her is a full grown
woman who has had
her share of playing ways.

Not afraid to let her
front door
hit you where she let
it miss you in meeting
you.
She won't do the child-like,
silly ways
No, not today.
Her mentality being one
that just won't except it.
Her Mindset in mindfulness is
at attention. Not stating she
will look for said deceit
in kiddie ways.
Trust in complete trust she
does possess
After it's shown that you
deem to be
trustworthy.
So the question is
Are you calculable.
Can she confide in you.

Depend on you.
Can she rely on you.
Are you in your very
being
able to be held accountable
for what your asking in her.
To do or provide what is
needed
and right.
Deserving of trust
Are you Worthy of her
honesty in love.
Because she is with all
definition definitely
worth it.

She's a one to put it all
out there
and deeply share,
in all her giving ways
She can tell you her fears
As with she you very well
can indeed.
When you can't sleep and
she's in deep
In her you can wake
Just to simply speak.
With her you can be
silent
Not say a single word
And she will be right

there.
All in with you.
Your faith, when yours
is gone
Pushing you in staying
on the righteous path.
Expecting in needing
the very exact thing.
These are her offerings
she simply bring, in
putting them on the table
out there in the very open.
Because one thing she
can and will not put up with
Is childish
Silly
Lying
Deceitful ways
Games

She Prayed For Thee

To say a prayer so deeply
and mean it with all that you
are, is how far in ways by
depth, her prayers for thee
simply are.
Along with her many others
Saying a prayer before she sleeps.
When she wakes as well as
Making her way through her
day to before she even eats.
Each and everyday is her heartfelt
prayer for thee
In hope that he's ok every minute
in all seconds throughout
each and everyday.

In wonder of whom he shall
be when entering the center
of her life. Knowing he to be
God sent is why she waits
so peaceful in her many
gracious behavioral ways.
As she simply may.
High respect with truthfulness
is what she possesses, for
self as she administers her
patience in deeply longing
of this benevolent way
in her waiting.

Sitting under a shade tree,
all of in a daze, sometimes
clouded with much haze
somewhat as a fog is how she
in times find herself embracing
when the mental plays in visions
come to head hitting her
right front and center.
Through knowing whom she
is and what she has in offering.
With much respect and love
for her very self.
Patience,
Love,
dedication,
and admiration
for self as well. Gives her the
strength by obedience that she
respectfully in-Depth truly
beautifully have.
In her pride in waiting.

In her many prayers she continues them throughout each
and everyday as she righteously,
wholeheartedly deeply pray.
As she prays for thee

Baby You Are

Baby you are the dew from
the trees,
You are the sun which
lights up my sky, when my
days are dark
You are the clouds that covers
me when it rains.
All of these things in all ways
is what you simply are to me.

Long walks with you, with
our tender lengthy talks are
everything that excites
intriguing me deeply.
Laying up with you doing
nothing else on this earth
other than in all of our essential
ways just all of being.
Us.
Nothing more than we.
Is all we have to be.

Laced by layers in our lovely
embraces you holding me
caressing the fullness of my
being, is all that of being deliciously beautiful to me.
Feelings of blue sky's and
bright rainbows is what I embrace when with you
completely

Deeply.
Mentally.
All in of our emotions.
A sentimentally emotional state.

To tell you that I Love You,
wouldn't touch the service to
what I in all ways with my whole
heart dutifully feel for you.
Yes it's my duty
One in which I've possessed
with so much aggression.
I will simply say in my little way
that when you were created, you
had to have been created exactly in specifics just for
me. Our hearts had to be on
the master plan to sync then
lock from the very beginning.
Each seemingly lost until our
beings became a one.
In which we in all definition
are.

To look me up in the Webster
you know where you will find
me. I can be found in the section
where it explains love in all of its
many elaborate details.
Yes that is where my heart
in all ways the matter truly
resides. When asked Baby what

you are.
This is unequivocally what
you are to me.

Feast On Each

So you say you want
a piece with some of this
magic in which she possess
in owning.
Are you sure you can
handle the tricks of
this in which she in mysterious
ways being
Meek,
Mild,
and profoundly reformed in
boldness with her stanzas
being from her
wants of more.
So as he is so peculiarly
tries to lay drip drops
of his masculinity on to
her enchanting being,
thinking he's ready for she.
Is he.
She smoothly in being
she all that of whom she
is.., her mental game.
Tho it's not one of which.
It's no game.
She waits.

He in all ways finally says in
admitting that yes it is in

fact her goodies in lyrics
he wishes to have a sample
of if she'd just only allow it.
See as she gathers she realizes
he simply believes that he and
she in their pieces in all ways
can be the shit.
All of that in flowing with him.
Who was he kidding.
All she withstood is what
it took to keep her from
loosing all her cool which
she'd been holding onto
for dear life.
He wanted her to just let it be.
But could she.
Not knowing him, blow with
him in smoothness

Succumbed to his
charmingly manly ways
she says
So you really wanna play.
In our outlays as they may.
Set on in his daring and bold ways
their mentalities go back and forth
on with their interesting intriguing plays.
Of lyrical, vocal out-pours to each of
their poetical images in imaginations.
His image to play such beautiful ballads
among within the tender keys which

withstood upon the elegant settings of
her mental sought out piano.
Of her being.
She laid out sheets of music in her
pieces as he gathered them each
word for word.
Finding himself drawn in more so
in more determination of wanting
their writings to be pen to pen.
He enjoys her flow the way she
goes , and wants to partake with
some of her floetic energy.

Still not quite sure by the actions
of his, she ponders within her elaborate
mental. Should she go with the flow
of it. Allowing her exquisite masterful
floetry to in-fact collaborate with what
he was bringing.
Following her gut, going with the way
she's intrigued by the way their energies
co-exist.
She takes him on in their sultry write
Teasing him as he to she. They both
in their wordings with so much elaborations
and mental simulations
mindgasms and thoughts
take on their ink,
pen to pen
deciding on going with the
beauty of it, they embark

on a lengthy
Feast On Each

The Night Before

As she lays the day away, she's
seemingly in her utter peace in-
between her cold sheets.
Laying bare in all her nakedness,
feeling the coolness from the nights breeze between every
sector of her nurtured nectar.
Brown thick, slick thighs, tight round ass,
breast quite succulent for a
gentle-mans seductive touch.
Upon lying their her mind
begins to wonder. As she ponders on the many ways
in the nights past she had her
man between those very sheets.
Her silk sheets.
Those being where she'd got her a good hard piece.

The million ways he simply moved her,
With his sex-tacy.
Eyes.
The sex he applied to her
hard earned body causing these
mental time lapsing moments of prolonged drawn out ex-t-
acy.
To play with the memory sends her cerebral into a state of
shock.
As she watches her clock somewhat mind blocked.
Counting the hours down to minutes to precious seconds
till she sees him all over again.
Just to do the delicious things they do.

The mindgasmed ways her mind craves when fed by her hungry mans cock.
She plays with that thought.
As she rests on the spot in which
they swayed only what felt like
a few hrs before.
She still feels him.
He has her like that.
Brain frozen goo-goo for the things which he do.

Closing her eyes she remembers
in searching, the way his hands
felt against her delectable sexiness.
So soft and gentle, they made her tremble beneath him so complete.
Remembering how whole she felt as their souls in all ways mindlessly met in connecting.
They had become one.
Over and over by time again
as he stroked her mind by erotically stroking
her deprived in her want from needing ebony body.
He had this special way in helping her embrace the fact that she with no doubts was a grown ass very hungry woman.
A one in whom with drawn out touch with all parts of her erotic sexy sex-u-ality.
She felt so freaky nasty the thoughts made her giggle.
She was proud.
Hell he did her in style.

Putting her core on this pedestal
in which he moved in every elicit way.

Definitely evoking these elaborate
images from feelings in pleasures of that she from so much
want bestowed within him. All about him.
He rocked her body hard. All night long.
Just the night before.

Bio:

Born Tameka Silver, in Longview, Tx she grew up from love in a single parent household. With a very loving mother whom supported all her hopes and dreams. She Graduated high school to go on in pursuing her life. She had her first child at the age of 18. Married at 21, where she had 4 more children with her husband.

Married 18 years to wake up one day finding herself in a marriage that failed. Accepting her parts by embracing whom she was as a woman.

From separation brought her peace. A solace In realizing by challenging who she was and who she is. In her discovery she took on by embracing being otherwise known as Meka La'Shun. Remembering writing poetry in her youthful days in embracing the peace from within made her realize she wanted to pick that passion for writing what was deep back up. Her therapy in quietness. Surprisingly, in her realizations she was discovered online one day by known author poet who helped her in putting her fears in her rear view. End results, she has embraced her gifts in writing poetry, collaborations, as well as short stories vowing to never fall back. Letting nothing stand in her way.

Motivated by inspirations she is on a journey of intellect. Embracing positivity.

www.ingramcontent.com/pod-product-compliance
Lightning Source LLC
Chambersburg PA
CBHW071626080526
44588CB00010B/1289